Parenting Boys

The Guide to Protecting Your Child With a Will and Trust

(The Essential and Practical Guide to Raising Children to Become Their Best)

Jeffrey Jackson

Published by Rob Miles

© Jeffrey Jackson

All Rights Reserved

*Parenting **Boys:** The Guide to Protecting Your Child With a Will and Trust (The Essential and Practical Guide to Raising Children to Become Their Best)*

ISBN 978-1-990084-25-6

All rights reserved. No part of this guide may be reproduced in any form without permission in writing from the publisher except in the case of brief quotations embodied in critical articles or reviews.

Legal & Disclaimer

The information contained in this book is not designed to replace or take the place of any form of medicine or professional medical advice. The information in this book has been provided for educational and entertainment purposes only.

The information contained in this book has been compiled from sources deemed reliable, and it is accurate to the best of the Author's knowledge; however, the Author cannot guarantee its accuracy and validity and cannot be held liable for any errors or omissions. Changes are periodically made to this book. You must consult your doctor or get professional medical advice before using any of the suggested remedies, techniques, or information in this book.

Upon using the information contained in this book, you agree to hold harmless the Author from and against any damages, costs, and expenses, including any legal fees potentially resulting from the application of any of the information provided by this guide. This disclaimer applies to any damages or injury caused by the use and application, whether directly or indirectly, of any advice or information presented, whether for breach of contract, tort, negligence, personal injury, criminal intent, or under any other cause of action.

You agree to accept all risks of using the information presented inside this book.

You need to consult a professional medical practitioner in order to ensure you are both able and healthy enough to participate in this program.

Table of Contents

INTRODUCTION 1

CHAPTER 1: SEPARATION AND DIVORCE WHAT NOW? 3

CHAPTER 2: PREPARING FOR VICTORY 12

CHAPTER 3: RAISE YOUR TODDLER THROUGH CONSCIOUS PARENTING 15

CHAPTER 4: SUPERMOM – TAKING CHARGE 22

CHAPTER 5: POSITIVE PARENTING SOLUTIONS 34

CHAPTER 6: ENCOURAGE THE CHILDREN TO SPEND 1 ON 1 TIME WITH NATURAL PARENTS 46

CHAPTER 7: NUTRITIONAL AND MEDICAL FACTS 49

CHAPTER 8: WHY DID THE ACTIVE LISTENING METHOD GAIN SUCH POPULARITY? 60

CHAPTER 9: UNDERSTANDING 65

CHAPTER 10: EFFECTIVE STRATEGIES FOR POSITIVE DISCIPLINE 77

CHAPTER 11: DISCIPLINING YOUR CHILD PROPERLY 86

CHAPTER 12: THE JUDGMENT OF OTHERS 95

CHAPTER 13: HOW PREGNANCY SETS THE OXYTOCIN TONE 116

CHAPTER 14: HOW TO BUILD A CONNECTION WITH YOUR CHILD☐ 125

CHAPTER 15: POSITIVE PARENTING WITH TODDLERS 141

CHAPTER 16: HOW TO BRING OUT THE BEST IN YOUR CHILD 152

CHAPTER 17: HOW TO RAISE A TEENAGER RIGHT 159

CHAPTER 18: DIFFERENCE BETWEEN BOYS AND GIRLS (PRESCHOOLER LEVEL) 171

CHAPTER 19: LEARNING THROUGH PLAY 175

CONCLUSION 193

Introduction

We all know that family is the basic unit of every society; the family in this case includes fathers, mothers and the kids. But even if it is true that a family is important, we all know that giving birth or siring children is a lot different from bringing them up and molding them to be responsible adults who can be looked up on. Do you ever stop to think that the way you could be interacting with your children even when they are toddlers could make a huge difference on whether they will grow to be responsible adults or not? Do you know that the manner in which you interact with kids will have a profound impact on their emotional and social wellbeing? In as much as babies don't come with manuals, knowing how to balance between showing them love and affection and molding them to face the world and not baby them is very important. Every father has a unique role to play in a baby's upbringing while the mother too has a profound role to play. Assuming that one parent will double as both is pure self-deceit. Mothers cannot be fathers and fathers cannot be mothers; history has already set a place for each parent so the earlier you take your place in a child's upbringing, the better for you and the child. This book will unravel the diverse parenting styles that fathers and mothers have and how to strike balance; you will be amazed by some of the things you will find about the importance of both parents in a child's life.

Chapter 1: Separation And Divorce What Now?

When two parents separate, children have no choice but to live with arguing, unreasonable grown-ups. If there are people who are more likely to suffer, they are definitely the children. They have no idea or interest in the rights and wrongs that led to the separation. Toddlers, given their age, cannot grasp the permanence of the situation and no matter how unreasonable one parent has been, they still wish to see their Mom and Dad together. Older children, on the other hand, only keep mum of the situation and just let their parents be.

Separation and divorce come with its share of problems. How these affect the child will only be dependent on the willingness of the custodial parent and the amount of support to be given to the children involved. So no matter how unhappy life has become after the break up and how emotionally shattering it is for the kids, a sole parent must learn to readjust and carefully tackle the following:

Custody rights – this often becomes the number one problem between fighting parents. Access rights must be kept open, can occasionally be restricted especially on cases where one parent is emotionally unstable, but should rarely be blocked. If the mother or father wants the custody be granted to them, they must be willing to do settlements. The bottom-line should be both parties must look after the welfare of the kids.

Money – going solo with mouths to feed would definitely bring a drastic drop in one parent's standard of living. This is all the more devastating especially if you see your ex husband or wife living a luxurious life and displaying relative abundance. When one parent picks up the kids for their scheduled visit, they may be feted and feasted, and then return after a weekend luxury to a parent scratching to make ends meet.

If you are a Mom and full custody to your kids has been granted to you, returning to work will do well to boost your morale and crushed self-esteem, but you need to ensure that your job pays well to be worth pursuing. Otherwise, you might want to concentrate on taking care of the kids and consider starting up your own business.

If you are a Dad and full custody to your kids has been granted to you, you have to realize that a father has the moral and legal duty to support his children. According to the law, child support is taken from a parent's salary especially the father's.

Should there be discrepancies in settling money matters such as a self-employed father contesting so the wife gets nothing or the custodial father got fired out from his job and relies on the ex-wife's child support leading to both parties becoming bitter of each other, the end result is that there are no real winners in a separation. So think about this possible scenarios before calling it quits.

Housing– this is another consideration as many families oftentimes make hasty decisions to gather up their belongings and leave home. Just a word of caution: avoid making decisions you will regret in the end. Apart from the financial burden brought by moving from one home to another, you will only add insult to the injury. Your children have already lost a complete family and losing this familiar place they call home will only double the pain.

Access visits – no matter how you take it, visitations are inevitable. You have the option to feel bitter about it and show it through your actions and reactions or take it without batting an eyelash. Of course it hurts when you see your ex taking your children for some weekend bonding while you wash, care, and feed them all week. But know that when you have agreed to separate, one of these luxuries are no longer in your control.

Sole parenthood is not always the husband cheating the wife or the wife leaving the husband. There were times when it is caused by an untimely death of a young parent. This is much more upsetting than would be news of an annoying divorce or separation. According to statistics, a child whose father has been killed in an accident stands to emerge emotionally many times sounder than the child of a long running divorce. Sad to say, parents do not know that they are causing more harm to their children by their deliberate actions than through life's unavoidable accidents.

Regardless of the situation you are into, both parents must take note of the following:

Your main priority must be the welfare and emotional well-being of your children.

Always consider the age of your children. Little ones need as little change as possible. Just leave the entire details to the older children.

If separation is the only option left, make sure that it is cordial and agreeable as possible.

Never underestimate the harmful effects of stress brought by the separation on your children. Assure them that Mom and Dad may be angry with each other, but they are not the reason of the frequent fights.

Toddlers show they are upset when they start being clingy and acting up. Young children are more intense in their reactions, while the older ones carry more of the burden but less obvious wound.

It must be explained well to your children that no matter what happens, they will still have two parents who will love and take care of them, only that you are no longer living in one roof.

They must be informed of where the other parent resides, their new home, and many other changes that will take place in the next days, months, and years to come.

You may be separated or divorced from your spouse, but your children should not be divorced from their grandparents who only wish their grandchildren well.

Never spy on the other parent. Respect each other's privacy.

Everything must be settled, from the custodial parent, access rights, education, and other amicable settlements for the welfare of the children.

Chapter 2: Preparing For Victory

There is a transition going on, and it is to your advantage if you know what is happening to your teenager. This is a difficult time for them. There is always a resistance to change because change removes us from a position of comfort. Make this transition easier for you and your teenager as you commit yourself to winning the battle to raise your teenagers as responsible and well-rounded adults.

Commitment Contract

First, here are few reminders before you proceed to the actual principles. You have to make a commitment that you will try to the best of your ability to follow these steps while you are in the process of raising your teens. Here they are.

1. Commit to loving your teenager come what may. Do not be torn between loving your teenager and hating their behaviors. Sometimes, parents make the mistake of getting angry at their kids because of their behaviors and actions. You can hate the behaviors and the actions that go alongside with those actions while still loving you teenager. They will know and feel the difference. Just keep on loving them, come what may. Love never fails. In the end, it will always prevail.

2. Have this mantra, "The teenage stage is just one season in our lives". This will keep you strong and positive when everything seems to be going against your plans and will. Reminding yourself that this is just a temporary phase will make you less anxious. There will be times when you will hear yourself ask, "when will this end?" Be comforted to know that there is indeed an end to all these dramas. Be calm, close

your eyes and repeat those sentences until you have inner peace. You would need this in the future, so practice as early as you can.

3. Always maintain your cool. It will do you good, and your teens will benefit from it, too. These are called the drama years. You are the one designated to stop the drama. You do this by being level-headed and calm. Avoid being hysterical at all cost. Keep your cool.

4. Remember that you were once a teen, too, and now, you are the responsible adult. So, the same can happen for your teens as well. Remembering how you were and how you were treated and what worked for you might help you. Do not forget, however, that each teenager is unique. There is no single formula that is guaranteed to work each time.

5. Never give up. You will be tested. You will feel frustrated, hurt and angry. There may come a time that you will just want to give up and let them be. Do not quit. Do not give up. This is not permanent.

The importance of your role as parents in guiding your teenagers during this time cannot be overemphasized. Your love and commitment are required to ensure victory in raising your teens so they can be the best that they could be.

Chapter 3: Raise Your Toddler Through Conscious Parenting

It requires ample amount of efforts and vitality to raise a toddler with complete efficiency and competence. However, these efforts prove to be fruitful and noteworthy when you find your child as a courteous and shrewd individual. We have provided hereunder some effective and remarkable suggested ways to bring up a toddler through conscious parenting –

· The most crucial thing that a parent is required to do is to spend quality time and talk to their kids. It has been significantly observed by the child experts that the more frequent talking taking place between the parents and the child leads to rapid growth of the kids in terms of learning rich vocabulary.

· It is sometimes difficult to teach the toddlers how to speak. It can be conveniently accomplished by narrating a story to them and you do this on a regular basis.

· Develop the effective habit of reading within your toddler kid by reading effective picture book for your kids.

· The emotional intelligence also plays a crucial role in the effective development of a toddler apart from language as well as vocabulary development. It is also responsible for the cognitive and social growth of the child. The best method to enhance the emotional intelligence of your kid, teach them to interpret various emotional cues.

· Teaching of various intentional and accidental activities to the children is also essentially required. By spending a quality time with your toddler, you can teach him or her, the difference between the accidental activities and intentional activities.

· Another distinctive method of building effective emotional quotient among your children is connecting them with various activities and actions. The best example of teaching through activities includes teaching them to say 'thank you' during the exchange of anything. Learning through activities proves to be a lifetime teaching for kids.

· One of the most widely spread and excellent conscious method of learning for kids is learning through playing. Various games are available for kids of toddler age group which offer significant leaning to them. However, it also requires a significant control and regulation of the parents while playing.

· An outstanding, designer and spacious ambience of the room also proves to be significant for the effective upbringing of a child. The toddlers can expand their motor and developmental skillsby fiddling with the toys littered in the room. It is akin of trial and error process.

· Choose exceptionally imaginative toys rather than smart toys to develop the ability of playing through experimentation within your child. Provide them with complete exposure to various creative activities like painting, dancing, music, building blocks and many more to enhance their creativity.

· The major cause of happiness for children of all age group is an appraisal coming from the parents. Appreciate their good deeds as well as their efforts to let them bloom. This will teach them the importance of efforts apart from intellect.

· Never keep your child into any kind of restriction. Let him become an extraordinary explorer by letting him play according to his choice. This will help in building an independent personality of your toddler.

· Always try to set forth higher standards of games for your toddler to motivate and encourage the feeling of striving harder which in return builds up a huge strength, spirit and confidence in him.

· Always teach your toddler from the beginning to be independent and flexible by letting them stand on their own whenever they fall down. Make it their habit to fall asleep and eat food on their own.

· Try to spend quality time with your toddler in playing, talking, and reading books to them instead of exposing them towards media devices. It is useful to involve themin more physical activities like jumping, running, catching and many more.Media devices like television can cause adverse effects on their development.

· Ensure proper balance of physical activities along with ideal sleep as it also proves to be a significant factor for child's development. Irregular kind of sleeping adversely affects the mental and physical health of the kid.

Chapter 4: Supermom – Taking Charge

No matter how daunting the task seems of taking charge, remember, you are the adult and no matter how smart your child may seem to you, you are still the one laying down the rule for your child to follow. When it comes to technology and raising a child in the internet age, parents are not able to take control over their children and their rising dependence on the internet for almost everything from homework to socializing.

Kids these days seem to be updated on the ever changing technology, and while they can make you feel inadequate while trying to set some rules for gadget usage at home, you could be called the bad guy. As a parent, I will only say this; you do know much more than you think. And you definitely know more than your child. Do not let your child lure you into allowing excess usage of any gadget or device at home.

It is only now that researchers in the education department are beginning to understand how exposing children to technology at an early age can lead to their development being affected as we have read in the previous chapters. Like every other parent, I wanted my child to grow up to be a better adult in the future, and I knew that because of me taking things very lightly and ignoring the symptoms which were right in front of me, I had to take charge of my kids and their addiction to my gadgets at home.

A growing number of software solutions are available which enable parents to keep a tab on their children's online activities. While you may consider this to be snooping, it isn't. Not when you know your child could be bullied online or is being affected by what websites he visits, especially if he is below 18 years of age. Experts however continue to advise that no application or software can help well than old school parenting techniques. Since we belong to a generation of parents who are raising millennial kids, on a daily basis we battles the pros and cons of the internet and devices which help us connect to the internet. While the use of phones has been banned within school premises, several children with their own phones find it more convenient to use their phone when in school. Two in four young children have experienced online/cyber bullying as per statistics in a report recently released.

Psychology experts have warned parents that children face the peril of being bullied for the way they look, as well as other concerns which need to be noted are privacy issues and relationship issues. Dr. David Fernandez recommends having time-outs and keeping restrictions on smart phones including the usage of Wi-Fi at home. Children often pick role models early in life, and depending on what they see, you need to ensure they don't want to be inspired by some advertisement online on how they can be skinny super models or clicking on any random links which can get them into trouble.

Another word was coined to explain the paranoia parents feel now a days with regard to their children leading most of their lives online rather than be physically present to have a chat with their parents – Juvenoia was coined from the words, Juvenile and Paranoia to describe the fear that parents feel about the internet and the social trends of having fancy gadgets which could have severe negative effects on a child's way of thinking.

If you think of it, as a parent, we are in quite a catch-22 situation. While parents do see the benefits of having the internet around and want their children to use technology, however at the same time we also want to dictate what our children can or cannot use a device for. School counselors have warned parents that no gadget can replace the bond shared by the parent and their children. However, since parents are so busy in trying to fulfill every wish and command of their children, there is no time left for any family interaction at home.

Psychologist Dr. David observes that with parents busy trying to work and deal with household work, they have no time left for parenting unlike old school parents where the mother was always there for her kids any given time of the day even if she was working. While many parents argue that the offline world is unsafe too, that does not give us reason to allow our children to get full freedom from any restrictions being imposed on them for all their online activities.

If you are still unsure as to how you can take charge as a Supermom and help lay down the rules, I have mentioned below some of the points which have helped me to keep the gadget addiction under control in my home.

Be Firm While Setting Priorities

As your kids keep getting older, they will be under severe peer pressure. Your child might want the latest gadget doing rounds in the market just because a classmate of his got one for his birthday and is declared to be the coolest kid in school. With so many choices available these days, as a parent, you need to understand their requirements. Focus on what it is that your child needs rather than what it is your child wants. Buy a phone which you feel is within your budget and which will make you feel comfortable about your child's security and privacy in the World Wide Web.

When your child is issued their driver's license, you do not buy them a fancy sedan before having them experience a second hand car, do you? It is the similar story with gadgets. Just because your child knows how to use a computer or your smart phone or tablet, does not mean that they get to own one. A basic phone will help you to keep in touch with them and also help reduce any risky behavior. You can even decide a plan for your child's phone if it is absolutely essential that he/she must use one. Several schools have issues notices to parents informing them about the banning of smart phones from being used in school during student class hours. Once you identify your child's needs from his wants, you will find your job as a parent much easier than before.

If your child needs to do some research or look up pictures for their class projects, allow them to use your gadget or electronic device which can help them. But do ensure that they are only using it for educational purposes and not fooling you into using it for socializing online.

You're In-Charge as the Supermom

While your child may argue that the price of a phone is cheap, do not fall for that argument just yet. As a contributor to the family income, you need to work out your financial condition before making a hasty decision of adding one more phone bill to the ever-growing pile of bills.

Most experts on parenting suggest checking your child's internet activity – especially children below 18 years of age. This allows you to have a family device which can be a computer, laptop or an iPad which can be used by one and all at home and is rooted to your own house.

Avoid feeling pressurized all the time by your child's demands. Don't feel guilty for not having given in to your son's whim of wanting to own an iPhone before he can even work on algebra problems in school. The money you save from buying him a regular working phone can be added to his college savings. In the end, only he will benefit from it.

A dear friend of mine, Joanne, mother of a six year old and a twelve year old, got her eldest child an iPhone for his twelfth birthday. However, while handing him his gift, she also ensure he read and understood the dos and don'ts of owning a fancy device which was to be used responsibly. He was also made aware of the consequence he would have to deal with if he did not follow the rules laid down. When I asked her why she would gift him something this expensive at his age, her reply was simple. She wanted him to learn responsibility and nurture him to grow into a healthy young lad who would know the difference between good and bad as well as learn how not to be ruled by technology. She also felt that since she did trust her eldest child to be responsible when she was away at work, maybe he could inspire her youngest child to follow in his footsteps. Joanne even made It clear to her child that if any of the rules were breached, she would take the phone away and he would then only be able to borrow it from her for a few minutes. He was made to give her all passwords to any social networking sites including his personal e-mail (Joanne vowed she wouldn't snoop on him) and he needed to answer the phone whenever he was out. Joanne also ensured he did not carry the phone with him to school at all and the phone was switched off and handed over to her every night before his bed-time.

Find Time to Converse

Use the internet and advancing technology as an opportunity for both, you and your child to learn and share about the digital world. Several schools teach children which websites can be useful for them for all their school work. You can visit those sites too or sit with your child and help him research for his homework. Not only will your child be happy that you are helping him out, you will also develop a lovely bond with him and it will last as a memory for your child to cherish in the years to come.

As a Supermom, you need to check if your child is being offensive or is bullying others online. Don't go yelling at them if you do notice something, but talk it out. Inform them no matter what they learn in school, everything that they share online is not always going to be safe and thus, they need to be careful. Your child should also learn to come and tell you if he/she is being bullied online. Let's face it, the online world can be cruel and if you encourage your child to come talk to you, you might just get to know even more about your child as well!

Chapter 5: Positive Parenting Solutions

Being a great parent requires a lot of attention and consciousness since your child has to grow as an individual in the best way possible under your guidance. You will never be able to teach your children if you are not a well-informed parent. Positive parenting solutions allow you to bring out the best in yourself and your child by always offering unconditional love in a structured, positive environment. This approach will not only be good for you and your child, but also for society as a whole as your child grows to be an exemplary citizen.

Kids learn how to behave by watching their parents. Demonstrate to them a positive character and they will grow up with a positive mindset as well. Always encourage your children to do the best in life and help them learn in the best way. Always appreciate the little things. When you are aware of your actions and words, it makes the home environment secure for the child, and they are able to learn with more flexibility. By implementing love, logic, and positive parenting solutions into your parenting routine you will raise an individual who not only meets your expectations and dreams, but meets their own.

Positive Parenting

The concept of positive parenting was first introduced by a Viennese psychologist. It emphasizes positive discipline with mutual respect for both the parents and the child. The primary focus is creating a clean future for the child where he/she is capable of sustaining themselves alone in the world. It focuses on mental growth, behavior, emotional health, academics and overall performance in the future as he/she grows up. It is the parent's responsibility to discipline the child and practice positive parenting techniques with the child regularly, so he/she is used to this approach. Here are some of the positive parenting practices which can help you in disciplining your child: Best Practices to Help Your Child Grow Positively

The following practices allow parents to focus on positive solutions when dealing with a wide variety of behavioral challenges.

1. Understand the Reason for Their Action
Whenever a child misbehaves, there is always a reason for their behavior which you need to understand as a parent. The question of "why" can be answered only by the parents because more often than not the child's behavior is a reaction to something negative you have been

portraying to him/her. Sometimes, when the child needs something really bad, and you respond harshly, that thought or aggression can stick in the child's mind and compel him/her to react unexpectedly in the same way later on. You have to understand the reason and connect the dots to recognize your child's emotions and address their feelings in a helpful way instead of getting angry.

When the parent is aware of the reason, he/she can deal with the child in the best manner automatically and calmly. Take the moment as an opportunity to teach the child the right way to behave in a situation where a negative reaction may be their default. When you respond in a calm manner, it will prevent her/him from creating or repeating the same action in the future.

2. Show Kindness and Firmness

As a parent, you have to be a role model for your child so make sure to show kindness towards others which can motivate them to do the same. Children always look up to their parents and modify their behavior accordingly, which is why it is necessary that you stay consistent with your practice while dealing with the people around you. When the parents are kind and firm, the child learns immediately to mimic the same attributes. Your kindness can help keep your child calm and cooperative with others in the present and future as well.

If your child becomes insistent about something, such as buying a toy or having another cookie, yelling is never the correct response. You can refuse them with kindness and firmness, without yelling. It is always better to keep your emotions under control and talk in a kind tone to help keep your child's behavior controlled as well. If you use a mean or harsh tone, then surely the reply will be negative as well. You do not have to be loud in order to convey the message. Instead, take the high road and choose to be kind to your child and handle them wisely.

3. Take Time Out

As a parent, it feels like there is no end to the demands being placed on you and no opportunity to take time out for yourself. Consequently, the stress builds up and comes out in front of your children. This is something which you should avoid at all cost. Be sure to take some time for yourself, even if it's only a few minutes. For example, if you are upset about something, then it is better to go in a separate room and sit quietly by yourself than to remain in the same room as your kids and risk taking your stress out on your kids.

Keep in mind that you have to teach discipline to your child so you have to keep your out of control emotions in check. If you are feeling too tired, then leave your child with the nanny or grandma for some time and relax for a few hours. It will help defuse your stress and you will be able to think clearly again. When you pick your child up, you will be in a happy mood which will have a positive effect on the child's behavior for sure. Tackle your issues on your end without even letting a hint of it reach the child.

4. Creativity Instead of Harsh Punishment

If you think punishing your child for a mistake will make them not do it again, then you are sorely mistaken. It does not fix the issue, and it leaves a bad impression on the child. Harsh punishment can create thoughts of revenge and rebellion which can produce no good byproduct. Instead of punishing your child, you can think creatively and respond with "positive time-outs." This means you can help your children getting out of the problematic situations which force them to behave negatively. You can also help your child learn to remain calm so that they can start practicing good listening skills.

You should never isolate, yell at, or spank a child if he/she misbehaves, because it will always cause reactionary behavior. Make every difficult situation with your child into an opportunity for you to use your own creativity to help your child in the best possible way. Stay flexible and try to be innovative with new ideas which can help your child grow into a better human being.

5. Show Consistency in Your Behavior
You have to be consistent in your

behavior, which should always be positive in nature. Positive behavior should not only occur just in front of the children, but also when you are alone or interacting with someone else too. You should always depict positive attributes. Most of the time when you are talking to someone in person or on the phone and you think your child is playing out of earshot, he/she can still hear you.

Do not talk about someone else in a negative manner or your child will think it's reasonable if they do the same. By staying consistent in your behavior you show your child that positivity is something which they need to adopt not just with people they are close with, but it should be part of their behavior all the time with everyone.

6. Understand Your Child

It is important that you think from your child's perspective. The prefrontal cortex part of the brain does not develop in a child until he/she turns three. So do not leave them with the impression that they have to face negative consequences for bad behavior.

Always help in redirecting or guiding so when they reach a point of understanding your actions, they will be able to build a positive personality. When a child begins to develop cognitive thinking, then you can give them logical reasons to help them better understand why a positive mindset is best, which can help modify their behavior even more.

7. Help Them Learn

You have to guide children step by step since everything is new for them. If you know something, that does not mean he/she knows it as well. To help your child learn, prepare a schedule and make it into a learning lesson every day with themed tasks such as cleaning day, eating healthy day, yardwork day and more.

Teaching them in small steps helps them learn how to tackle challenges and eventually prepares them to problem solve on their own when they are older.

Help your child when it's necessary, but let them do the majority of the work. If he/she does something wrong, demonstrate the correct way to do it and do not get angry at any point. Communicate well, and you will see how easily they will learn.

8. Stay Very Patient

Parents have to be patient with their children if they want to see good results in their behavior later on. When you are guiding your child to keep their behavior positive, then the most important attribute is your own patience. Once you gain control of your own emotions, you will see the effects of it in the later stage of the child's life, which will make all the hard work worth it.

Chapter 6: Encourage The Children To Spend 1 On 1 Time With Natural Parents

Never come between your step children and either one of their parents. Encourage them to spend time alone with each of them. Do not feel like this is any kind of a threat to you. If you have children, you know how special that time you spend with them is to you and to them.

It is very important for the children to maintain some regularity and consistency in their lives. Things are changing for them in so many ways, and just because you are trying to build a new family structure, they are not putting their former family behind them.

When you encourage them to spend more time with their natural parent(s), you are showing them that you accept that they love their parents and that it is okay with you. No one is trying to take the other parent's place in their lives. There is room enough for all.

Allowing and encouraging your step children to nurture the relationship they have with their parents will earn their trust, respect, and love will follow. It doesn't happen overnight; but with time and patience, your new little family will be an important place for them to feel respected and loved too.

It is always paramount that you and your spouse NEVER speak in negative terms about either one of your exes in front of the children. Always respect the other parent, no matter how bad your relationship with him or her is. Children love both of their parents, and putting them in the middle of your "war" with your ex is not healthy for anyone. Not only will this make a child lose respect for you, but it will also provide a basis for the child's ability to play one parent against the other, including the step parent.

When all of the parents are able to put their own feelings aside and work together for the children's sake, that is when you all will have success with helping your children grow into responsible adults, while feeling loved and respected by all of their parents, step parents included.

Chapter 7: Nutritional And Medical Facts

Children require proper nutrients for growth and health. Children also require proper medical treatment. It is your responsibility to ensure that your children receive proper nutrients and medical treatment. We have discussed the importance of parents maintaining proper nutrients and medical care so that you are at the top of your game and able to properly care for your children. Now, we will discuss how to provide nutrition and medical care for your children to make them healthy and function at their peak performance level.

As an infant, your child remains on formula or breastmilk until your doctor advises you to begin introducing baby food and eventually solid foods. Once your child becomes a toddler, the real dietary challenge begins. You may notice that your toddler becomes a picky eater. He may refuse foods that he once loved. This is normal. However, making sure that your child gets the proper nutrients at this stage in life is vital and has a massive impact on his development and health. A child's development in the early stages of life have a direct impact on their future development and overall health.

A guide to proper toddler serving sizes are as follows:

Milk and Other Dairy:

☐ Servings per day: 16-20 ounces of milk

☐ Low fat milk, soy, or rice milk is recommended. Other dairy product equivalents: ½ - ¾ ounces of cheese = 4 ounces of milk, ¼ cup of yogurt = 2 ounces of milk.

Fruits and Vegetables:

- Servings per day: 5+
- Serving sizes: 2 tablespoons

Grains:

- Servings per day: 3-4
- Serving sizes: ½ slice of bread, ¼ cup of cooked or dry cereal, ¼ cup of pasta, or ½ tortilla

Meat and Protein:

- Servings per day: 2
- Serving sizes: 1 ounce of fish, lean beef, pork or chicken, ½ egg, 2 tablespoons of beans or legumes, or 1 tablespoon peanut butter.

As your child grows, his serving sizes will grow with him. It is recommended that you introduce new foods regularly into your child's diet to so that mealtime is less boring, and your child is introduced to a variety of different flavors over the years. You will soon find that your child enjoys a wide variety of healthy foods. This will set a pattern in motion that should continue throughout your child's life of eating healthy and enjoying a healthier lifestyle.

Just as proper diet and good eating routines assist in creating future healthy eating habits, a poor diet in childhood will create poor eating habits in your child's future. A poor diet can exist because of numerous factors. One factor is denying your child the proper nutrients to obtain maximum health. Another factor is allowing your child to consume unhealthy amounts of sugar and fats. Finally, a factor in many poor diet habits are linked to parents allowing their children to over-eat and consume larger portions of either healthy or unhealthy foods. Just as with an adult diet, children consuming much larger amounts of certain nutrients can be harmful to their health and development.

When shopping for food, it is always best to go without your children. When shopping alone, you can concentrate on what you need. If your child is shopping with you are more likely to purchase items, such as junk-foods, just to pacify an unruly child. You are also more likely to be distracted and forget the items you need.

When shopping for meats, look for meats with little or no fat. Saturated and trans fats have long been directly linked to high cholesterol and heart disease. When purchasing red meat, look for the words "round", "loin", or "sirloin" to identify leaner red meats. Always trim any visible fat from the meat you are cooking and drain the fats that cooks out of the meat after it is cooked. Eat a minimum of processed meats like ham, bacon, sausage, and hot dogs. Finally, cook all meats in the healthiest manner possible, including baking, broiling, and roasting the meat.

Read all labels when you are shopping for nutritional foods. Many of the foods you think are healthy may contain high amounts of sugar and others may have little to no nutritional value. Do your homework before you go shopping. A quick guide on how to read food packaging labels can easily be found online. Once you have a good understanding of how companies label the ingredients and nutrients on their labels you can easily make a more informed decision about what you are feeding your family. A responsible parent knows what they are feeding their children.

Finally, make sure you go grocery shopping at the right time. The ideal time to shop in your local grocery store is when there is the least traffic in the store. An over-crowded isle can make you feel rushed and cause you to overlook needed items. However, many of us shop when time allows us to shop. Also, never go shopping for food when you are hungry. Every unhealthy item looks inviting and mouth-watering when we are hungry.

Breakfast is the most important meal of the day. Your child will be more alert, do better in school, and have a better attitude if he eats a balanced breakfast. A balanced breakfast includes eating foods from four of the five recommended daily food groups: dairy, grain, fruit, and meat. When you are rushed and do not have the time to prepare a full course breakfast for your children or your children want a change, cereal or oatmeal with a serving of fruit is a good substitute. Make sure the cereal and oatmeal you have in your pantry is a good source for grains and has a low sugar content.

Your child's evening meal should be no later than 7:00 p.m. Children should never go to bed hungry or on a full stomach. The evening meal should contain foods from each of the five basic food groups: dairy, grains, fruits, vegetables, and meat. As with any other meal, portion control is important for the evening meal. A good rule of thumb is to dispense portions of each food group in a size no bigger than your child's fist. Even the leanest and healthiest of foods can cause unhealthy weight gain if consumed in large proportions.

As with yourself, your child needs regular checkups. Even if your child has not been sick or showing any indications of any illnesses, there are basic testing and examinations that pediatricians conduct that can detect issues that may cause your child medical issues later. Between the typical annual checkups, parents must use good judgements as to when they are to seek medical attention for their child. All children get sick, but every childhood ailment requires medical attention. If a child has pains that do not subside within a few hours you need to seek medical care. If your child has a high fever that does not subside and continue to reduce with the use of over-the-counter medications, you need to seek medical care. If your child has a discoloration or abnormal coloring of the skin, eyes, or fingernails, or if your child has any symptoms that cause you to be concerned about their health, seek medical attention.

All children need to be vaccinated against certain diseases. These vaccinations start when the child is around three months old. Once your child has been fully immunized and vaccinated against these diseases, the vaccinations will weaken over time. There are required boosters that are given to children at specific ages to keep their immunity strong against these diseases. It is the responsibility of the parents to keep up with these shots and know when it is time for the booster shots. Many parents choose to use their local Health Department for these kinds of shots because they have a good system of keeping track of the child's shots and many send the parents notifications when they are due for more shots.

As with yourself, if your child's healthcare coverage is provided through an assistance program, you owe it to your child and the taxpayer to keep your child healthy and to provide him with proper nutrients and care.

With today's society becoming more and more dependent on prescription drugs, it is recommended that you ask your doctor if your child's condition can be treated with non-addictive drugs when having to take prescribed pills or liquids. Make sure you advise your child's doctor of any known allergies and any medications (even over the counter and supplements) your child is taking for any reason. Make sure you advise your doctor of any known allergies and medical conditions. This information helps the doctor to determine the best course of action when treating your child and prescribing needed medications.

Chapter 8: Why Did The Active Listening Method Gain Such Popularity?

When parents start trying to listen actively, and these reflexes begin popping up very quickly in their speech, the children themselves feel surprised. They instantly think that they live better now, start behaving differently, and be more attentive to their parents.

The easiest way to master active listening is to repeat the child's phrases after him. Of course, before repeating, they should be somewhat modified; otherwise, the child will quickly see through such apery. And then, instead of actual contact, we'll receive something else, such as the status of a clown, or, at least, of an extraordinary person.

However, if you need time to gather your thoughts, the following option will be an excellent continuation of the conversation,

'You say that you won't go to school...'

We don't show any sympathy for the child, but we demonstrate that we've heard him. And we wish to continue the conversation. And be sure that he will tell you about his troubles because WE ARE WILLING TO LISTEN.

Usually, repeating your interlocutor's phrases, while being so primitive, is a highly efficient method. It's personal attractiveness lies in the ease of its use. Agree, it's much harder to determine what the child feels and adequately respond to his emotion, than copy his last phrase. The excellent point here is a tone, for if we imitate absently, among other things, we'll only spoil everything. Nor should we use the interrogative intonation. The question is often interpreted as an idle interest but not as sympathy. What about the positive tone, it is welcome: maybe you haven't guessed the emotion strictly, but you demonstrate the understanding of your child.

A few other things. It would seem that it's unfair to apply some crafty techniques in communication with your child. It's essential to communicate. Sincerely. And can we talk about sincerity, if we have to pick up every word, to build every phrase? When you don't pay much attention to a child for the first time, you instead pay it to terms and manner of speaking. Of course, it hinders you. Like crutches block someone who walks perfectly without them.

The first steps in active listening are not so easy. Some constraints, some false notes can always be seen. You have to think about something; you have awkward pauses... But this happens only for the first time. And then...

Then, the MIRACLE happens. The child opens to us, and we start understanding him. Not only understanding, however — we begin experiencing the beautiful feeling of kinship, unanimity, and our love for him starts playing with new colors.

But one will have to do his best to overcome oneself, one's stagnation, habits, laziness, and inertia, at least, to try.

At the same time, one should remember that active listening is just one of the techniques used only in an individual situation. In the case when the child needs to be heard, and, when at the same time, he is afraid that parents won't take his feelings seriously. This method works if some communication difficulties have already occurred in the family. And if a child tells all the news right out of the gate, and if you can't cease this speech flow, is there any point in pushing him?

Active listening is an incentive used only when needed!

Its constant use is not just unnecessary; it's even harmful. You don't have to break anything. Let your communication proceed as usual. It is essential not to overlook a situation when you need to apply active listening. And you can use it in such specific cases. Anyway, active listening is a handy tool. And it will facilitate your life significantly provided that you use it appropriately.

REMEMBER: THE WAY YOU ADDRESS THE CHILD, THE CHILD WILL SEND YOU, ACCORDING TO THE LAW OF IMITATION. Children apply imitation. So, if you say '**no, you won't,**' he will answer, '**no, I will.**' He is mirroring and reflecting you. '**I will punish you**' - '**Well, go!**'. While applying directive methods, it won't be easy to take into account all child needs. And the same is true for husbands and wives. Do you think you can make your husband or wife do something? No. What children start doing? Cheating parents. Just like adults in everything.

Chapter 9: Understanding

Understanding between parents is incredibly important when using the principles of positive parenting. Parents need to understand and be understood in order to raise children who have a capacity to show love, respect and understanding towards others. To be a positive parent, some self-examination may be required. You will need to know who you are and what you know. You may also need to reinvent who you are or make changes to your own habits.

A large part of being an effective parent is knowing how to read your child. You need to understand what they are thinking and why. Can you look at your child and just know they are being honest? Can you know without a second thought what your child is thinking? If you are someone who can read body language and facial expressions easily, that will help you become a better parent. Even if you're not an expert, you'll be able to get to know your child's body language as they grow.

Here is an example:

A highly independent child, a young girl, approaches her mother with a question. She doesn't normally seek help for her problems and she has agonized over both the question and the situation. However, she figures that her mother knows best. When she asks her mother, there is anxiety in her voice but her mother was busy working when she asks. Her mother doesn't give her daughter the attention and so, doesn't see or hear the anxiety her daughter is expressing. The mother gives a short answer but does not explain her response. This leads to the young girl to think that her problems are not important or important enough for her mother.

This example illustrates how important it is for you to engage and be attentive to your child's body language. If you do not, it is possible to miss important cues that may cause your child to feel unsettled or to feel unimportant. This feeling could be monumental to your child and all because of some missed signals. You do not want to miss all the cues.

Body Language Exercise

You can do the following exercise on your own, your child does not have to be present. Visit a public park or other public place and find a spot to sit down. You do not need to interact with anyone, for now you are just there to observe. If you need to, record what you see in a small notebook. The important thing is to observe the interactions of other people.

Writing down what you see can be a great way to look back on the things you observed and remember or analyze them. With time you may remember other visual cues and come to a completely different understanding of the behavior than originally observed.

For example, let's say you are in a restaurant. There is a couple at a table beside you and they are talking heatedly. You only catch a few words but you can see that they are both upset. They are frowning at each other and it is easy to see they are angry. However, think about the other people in the restaurant. Is it not possible that others are also having a bad day or are angry too? Some people may be neutral in their expression but their body language says otherwise. They may have crossed arms or tension in their body. This is a good example of reading body language.

As you can see, body language can tell us a lot if we know how to read it. The first step is simply going out and observing other people. The next step is to start studying more about body language and facial expressions. To help you with this, you can use images online that assign emotions then explain how the face may move to show these emotions.

Understanding What is Said

Words are important and carry weight but that can also be misleading. There is a statement, "your words can lie, but your body can't." This statement is true for most people so when someone is talking, take their words to heart but also observe how it is being said.

As a parent, you have to listen and watch for the intention behind a statement or how a statement is being said. You know that it is very easy for children to adopt sarcasm or reply in a short way that is disrespectful. Always listen for these cues and head them off before it becomes a habit.

For this exercise, listen to conversations. You may want to write them down or even record them (with permission) to help you later.

Now, without looking at the person speaking, try to determine what the words truly meant. As the person is speaking, examine their face and body language.

Do you think you interpreted the words correctly?

If you need additional help, you can find videos or online aids for this exercise but if you can't find any that are useful, try watching foreign films without subtitles. There are some pretty great actors and actresses in other countries, particularly in Asian films, where showing emotion is more reserved.

When you watch a foreign film without the words, you have to try and follow the plot without an understanding of what is being said, thus the body language, facial expressions, and small mannerisms will have to be your cues.

Allowing Your Child to Learn and Understand

Your child needs to learn these concepts just as much as you do. A parent that has studied psychology and has a natural affinity for psychology tends to be able to provide more understanding but that doesn't mean you can't learn to do the same things yourself. You'll just have to learn the concepts quickly rather than by applying them over your entire life.

Understanding your child is just as much about how you react and communicate as it is about assessing your child based on their body language and words.

One key to helping your child understand you is by providing them with explanations for the reasons behind your actions. If you have reasons for the things you do and tell your child, not only does it help them feel included, but it will also show them your point of view.

Children are naturally creative and have active imaginations. Sometimes they may even have beliefs or ideas about things that aren't true or they may hold onto these ideas because they want them to be true. These beliefs may be harmful if it causes them to do things that are dangerous. It is important to understand how your child perceives a certain activity in order to help them understand why they should or shouldn't do it.

For example, if you tell your child not to touch the stove use their understanding of danger or being hurt to explain why. Tell your child, that a stove is hot and should not be touched. However, if your child wants something that isn't inherently dangerous, you need to have sound reasons for denying them that desire.

For example, your child wants to go to another school because they think it is better or all their friends go there. You have to explain to your child that those reasons are not good enough to change schools. That may be hard for them to understand because this is a "want", rather than a need.

Your child will learn these techniques when you provide understanding and reasons for your actions. Communicating is essential to helping your child understand the reasons behind your behavior and it will also help them gain more critical thinking. It will also give you an opportunity to respond to a problem before it becomes an issue or attitude.

Also, it is incredibly important to understand the situation. Sometimes outside factors can contribute to your child having a poor attitude, things like being hungry or tired.

Hunger is a big factor, in fact. A child who hasn't been given adequate meals or snacks will be hungry before dinner, that is obvious. They are also bound to be less than cheerful in their attitude because of hunger. Hunger makes all of us feel off or not as "with it". It can also shorten our patience and make us quicker to anger. Putting your child in a situation where they are hungry is naturally going to provide a problem. So instead of allowing hunger to contribute to a poor response from your child, provide a proper solution. If you are not home, you should always have snacks. It is the same if your child is tired.

A tired child is more likely to have tantrums or an overall poor attitude complete with complaints, anger and sometimes even tears. To help matters, try to get your child to take a break or relax, you may not be able to get your older child to nap, but there is every possibility that you can get them to relax and sit quietly.

You can also set yourself up for success by paying attention to the time of day. When it comes to the afternoon or the time when your child runs out of energy, use this natural down cycle to do something calm or quiet like reading a book. This can be the perfect opportunity to bond with your child too, you can read a book to them or sit with them while they read. Your child will be entertained and you know they are relaxing to recharge. This will avoid a lot of common negative behaviors because you have understood their need to rest before play continues.

Chapter 10: Effective Strategies For Positive Discipline

The use of positive discipline is an essential element for children. It will teach the child changes must be made when he/she has gotten into trouble for stepping outside of the realms of what is an acceptable situation.

The parent must use active listening and provide redirection so the child will understand why a particular behavior is not acceptable. You will most likely hear some strong emotions and a few tears, but you must remain calm and firm. When the smiles are gone; the child will realize lines have been crossed.

The Strategy

Setting limitations for a child is a critical step in parenting. The focus has to remain on significant elements with an appropriate limit in place to dissuade the child from poor conduct. It is important to discuss these limitations as much as possible with the youngster, so the rules are clearly understood.

The extent of the communication and comprehension will depend on the of the child's age. You can never start too early. The tones used during these conversations will be soothing to a child no matter what the age. For an infant, the parent could be speaking about today's chores, but the child will hear the even tones and feel secure.

An effective system of discipline will include three vital elements:

1) An environment categorized with an optimistic, loving, and supportive child-parent relationship

2) Strategic or proactive teaching and strengthening methods for desired behaviors

3) A reactive strategy to eliminate the undesired behaviors of the child

Each of these elements must be present to create a well-disciplined child, no matter what age group. If you child is doing something such as looking at a book which is inappropriate for his/her age; it is best to ignore it for the moment.

The child's attention span won't last for long. It is best to nonchalantly remove the book when the child releases it. This procedure goes back to picking and choosing the arguments. The child isn't in danger, and the book is just a passing item in a list of what the child has to do during the span of one day.

The One Minute Approach

When your toddler has pushed all of the buttons, and your temper is rising, you can take a few simple steps within the first minute to cool-down.

Step 1: React to Danger

Wait for about ten seconds before you respond to the misbehavior because you must remove the possible dangerous element from the situation. If your child found a pair of scissors and wanted to trim the puppy, you should approach slowly.

Never try to jump too quickly and make the matter worse than it already is.

Step 2: Remain Calm

Stay calm for about ten or twenty seconds and resist the urge to react hastily. It is usually an automatic reflex to yell, but the loving approach will work more effectively. Simply say, "May I have the scissors?" using a calm and collected voice. The pleading approach will signify a problem to the toddler but not an alarm to make him/her jump quickly and cause injury to both participants.

Step 3: Access the Problem

After about thirty seconds, you are ready to access what has happened and what can be done about the problem. Focus on what just transpired and not another incident of the same type that could or might have happened on another day.

Your child might not remember the incident, and you could be making a simple problem much worse. Try to stick to the current offense and ask if the situation could have been handled differently. Don't harp on the past, but repeat yourself as much as needed to ensure the child remembers and understands this is a form of discipline.

Step 4: Discuss the Consequences

Punishment is not always the correct answer. It is beneficial to talk to your child about what just happened. Questions should be asked, even with a young toddler. Children have a unique way of letting a parent know why he/she did the deed (right or wrong).

How severe is the crime? Was it sneaking a plate of cookies or grabbing a hot plate?

The punishment or reprimand needs to match the crime/threat.

Questions should be asked why he/she did not ask for the goodies, but it should be asked in a composed and stern voice, so the child realizes it isn't a game. Misbehavior is a serious issue. At the same time, you should not laugh and lead the child to believe it was a funny situation. Children learn much of his/her information from observation.

Step 5: Respect and Setting the Limits

Limits must be placed on toddlers for his/her health and safety as well as self-control issues. Issues are faced by parents from infancy and continue throughout the toddler years. Each child develops or learns at different paces. You need to know how to handle situations such as your children losing the pacifier, toilet training, and abuse/hitting other children or animals.

Children can learn from individuals who are directly in contact with them on a regular basis. Parents and caregivers are the role model and should offer respect to the child. Therefore, if you lose your temper, you should apologize.

Teach the Golden Rule at an early age for the child to treat others as he/she would like to be treated. When you practice the rule, the child will blend the logic into his or her future.

Demonstrate Using Fictional Characters

Toddlers love to play with puppets, and you can make your own version to display how the child is misbehaving or behaving. You can use Popsicle sticks, spoons, or paper plates to make your character.

Many children love to watch and listen to the silly sounding drama made by the puppet show actors, and the show will allow them to see how he/she looks and sounds during bouts of temper. It is always worth a try—besides—it could be a fun event for the child.

Granted it isn't necessary to give tokens to a child as a reward for good behavior, but you could try using the option of the 'fairy' left you a present for such good behavior. By providing a present from the 'fairy', you will not be seen as using a bribery technique to receive good behavior. The worst that can happen is the child discovers there is no fairy. At that point, simply explain the fairy left one final gift and moved away.

Choose Age-Appropriate Consequences

Parents have two types of enforcement techniques; removal and impositions. Removal is self-explanatory such as a time-out session. If the behavior has warranted a time-out, you need to be sure the toddler is old enough to understand why he/she is made to spend time alone without any of the special toys and possessions.

Most toddlers are too young to comprehend an imposition occurs when a parent doesn't allow you to attend a special function because of poor conduct. The imposition method becomes more effective with children who are a bit older and have passed the toddler stage.

Chapter 11: Disciplining Your Child Properly

Disciplining your child is as important as cuddling with them. It is another way for you to show them that you love them. If you discipline your child, you are telling them that there are limits, and children need limits. You are setting the tone that you are the parent and they are the child and that you make the rules, not them. It is essential to establish this important statement within your parent-child relationship as early as possible in your child's life.

Setting up boundaries with your child, is going to make them feel secure. By knowing what to expect, depending on their behavior, the child will learn right from wrong. Different sets of rules and discipline should be set for different group ages. Don't worry, if you feel at times like your child is testing you, this is absolutely normal. They all do it. Additionally, they will sometimes go back and forth between the two parents to see if they are playing by the same rules. It is important for this reason for the couple raising the child to be consistent as this will avoid one of the parents losing respect or being labeled as being "easy".

You will read below some proven and suggested discipline techniques. You should use different techniques depending on the age of your child and the severity of the incident or situation you are dealing with. In any case, the very first step is to sit down with your child, age permitting, and explain the rules of the house and the consequences if the rules are not followed. Try to make this a win-win situation. You are all living together, and if everyone behaves in an acceptable manner, it's easier for all and there will be no need for punishment.

Toddlers (3 years old and under)

Before the age of 6 months, there is obviously no discipline necessary. However, you should not hesitate to comfort your child when he needs you. Contrary to popular opinions, you can't spoil a child with love and being attentive to his needs.

Next, you can start to intervene as your child starts to develop his individual personality. You can substitute the spoon with which he throws food all over the floor, and replace it with a hard cookie to chew on (this is called redirecting). You should keep him safe as he is crawling and discovering the house, and always explain to your child what you are doing and why, even if they are very young because one day they will understand.

Next it's time to start reinforcing some basic rules like respecting nap and meal times. Use positive reinforcement each chance you get. If your child is listening well and straightening up the toys, reward him with a longer story at bed time. Then, closer to 2 years old, the child can be taught to take responsibility for his actions and clean up the mess he has made. You can teach your child to take turns using toys with his friends and the term "No" can be introduced, but you should try to always acknowledge your child's feelings while reinforcing the rules. As your child gets closer to 3, you can expect him to respond more receptively to orders. It will also be the start of the temper tantrum period. You should try to deal with their temporary anger crisis by trying to comfort them. They are upset about something and it's either valid or not. Sometimes a hug is all it takes to make everything better. Also, once the child turns 2, you can slowly introduce the time-out concept. Make sure you warn them before hand, maybe with a countdown (i.e. 3, 2, 1), and then give them a 1 minute time out per year of age. It's very important that you ignore the child's behavior while he or she is in time out, as long as they are sitting down. This can be a very effective method of discipline until the age of 7 or 8.

3-8 years old

The period between 3 and 8 years of age is a critical time in your child's development, and it is during this period that you can utilize the Reserve and Rewards Method. The main idea is to give a reward if the child behaves well, and they get the reward taken away if they are behaving badly. A great idea is to have a rewards jar, and the child must accumulate 3 stickers to in order to get a reward equivalent to 3 good behaviors. If they behave badly, they will lose a sticker and must wait longer for the reward.

Next it's time to prepare your child to deal with real life experience. If your child breaks or spills something in the house because they were horse playing, don't punish them. Instead have them clean up the mess.

It is also a good idea to try to give your child chances to correct his behavior. If your child screams hurtful words to his brother, intervene and ask him to think about what he said. If he can reword his feelings and apologize, you can avoid a dramatic evening and teach both your children a valuable lesson.

8 years old and up

Your child is getting older, so you can now begin to use different methods of discipline. Two of the more commonly used methods are grounding and withholding privileges. For example, if your child usually has freedom to play outside with his friends every day after school, he can be told to stay inside. The number of days or hours you will ground your child depends on the offense. Losing privileges works especially well with older children. Teenagers will feel completely lost without their computer or cell phone and might think twice about disobeying you in the future.

By following these simple disciplinary methods and keeping your child informed that there are consequences for bad behaviors, you are teaching them valuable life lessons. You want to prove him that respect is mutual and earned, and if he does respect you, you will do the same. Also, life is not always fair, so don't be afraid to disappoint or upset your children. They will have to learn to deal with frustrations in their life, so they need practice. Finally, the best gift you can give your child regarding discipline is to be consistent. They will then know what to expect and what to do to earn your approval, and stay out of trouble.

Chapter 12: The Judgment Of Others

Georgiana, a suburban mother of a two-year-old, was cooking supper when she realized that she didn't have milk. It was late March and about forty degrees outside. As her daughter had recently discovered the art of removing all of her clothes and was therefore nearly impossible to keep clothed, Georgiana decided to forgo the coat in favor of a blanket. She got in the car and went to the store.

She paid for the milk and was leaving the store when a middle-aged woman wearing lipstick and perfect curls eyed her toddler wrapped in a blanket. She gave Georgiana the stink eye as she watched her walk to her car.

Georgiana was irritated. After all, a child is hardly going to get hypothermia in forty degree weather. Obviously this woman had never tried to put a coat on a child who was more excited about removing clothing than she was about staying warm. Georgiana blew out a loud breath and returned home.

Georgiana pulled into the driveway and saw a cop in her waiting. Panic flashed through her. Had she accidentally left the stove on? Had there been a burglar? Had something terrible happened to a family member? Had she accidentally shoplifted? She rushed to the front stoop, toddler and milk in arms.

The officer barked questions at her and told her that he had to search her house. She watched the officer search every room in her house and inspect her child, who ran to play happily with a measuring cup on the floor.

Georgiana was furious and humiliated. What right had that stink eye woman to look at her and assume that because her kid was wearing a blanket in place of a coat she was being abused and neglected? Had the woman tried parenting a small child before? Didn't she understand that wrapping the squirming kid in a blanket was so much quicker than attempting to get her arms in the right holes of a jacket, a jacket which would be removed with rapid enthusiasm if Georgiana set her down for half a second?

When the police officer left, Georgiana returned to cooking supper, but the tears rolled. The fact that others thought she looked incompetent enough to call the police on her hurt. Was she really screwing up so badly? Was she a bad mother?

This story is a perturbing example of the power the judgment of other people can have. There are a million voices out there telling you that what you're doing is going to screw your kids up, or worse, that you have already screwed them up. On any given day, there is never a shortage of people ready to call you out, saying that they would do it differently and better.

Some days you feed Norah and Max chicken nuggets and cheerios straight from the box. One of them won't wear shoes while the other won't wear a coat. When you leave the room for a minute to do the dishes, they start smacking each other and running to you to tattle. To top matters off, you only had time to put eye liner on one eye, so you look like a crazy person who shouldn't have been allowed to reproduce. On these days, you're afraid that the judgment being heaped on you is not far off base.

People will judge you for doing, saying, or buying any number of things when it comes to your kids. They'll judge you for not breastfeeding just as quickly as they'll judge you for breastfeeding in public. Rachel, a new mother commented, "Some people actually got offended when I fed my infant in a restaurant. I was using a blanket and everything. There was nothing to see! I don't understand how a newborn baby eating could possibly be more offensive than, say, a teenage boy. Have you seen some of them eat? And no one locks them in a closet."

There are enough reasons for people to cast judgment on you that it can make your head swim. You chose not to put your four-year-old into dance class or piano lessons? Someone will judge you for that. You let your kid watch an hour of TV every day? Someone will judge you for that. You couldn't breastfeed or have a natural birth? You must not love your baby as much as everyone else. You are choosing to take your children to Sunday school every week? You let your kid play in the mud? You bought off-brand chicken noodle soup? You aren't wearing make up? Your infant isn't wearing shoes? You ignored your kid when she said something stupid that she's already told you six hundred times in the last hour? You must be selfish. You can't please them all. Trying to do so will drive you crazy—not a good result when you're trying to raise emotionally stable offspring.

Stephanie, a single mother of two children says, "Parenting makes me want to use swear words a lot more often than I ever did before, but I refrain because I know that if my children are the first ones using those words on the playground, it will reflect poorly on me and ensure that my kids are left out of all the birthday invitations."

Similac recently launched an advertising campaign that addressed this very issue called "The Sisterhood of Motherhood." In it, moms and dads from all walks of life and parenting styles from the breast feeders to the stay at home moms and dads to the working moms to the yoga moms are shown gathered around a playground. They make mean digs at each other's parenting choices and lifestyles. At the end, a baby stroller starts sliding down a hill, and all of them forget their insults to race after the infant in danger. The message (besides buy Similac formula, obviously), is that parents are parents first. Sadly, parenting doesn't usually tie up into such a neat, affirming bow.

Fear of judgment can have a lot of power over you, especially when it comes to the discipline of your children. Never underestimate the power of parenting fads and paranoid neighbors.

How the Fear of Judgment Undermines Your Effectiveness as a Parent

When you fear what others will think of how you are raising your kids, you can undermine your own discipline. To some of you, this may seem obvious, but for many of us, an explanation is warranted.

For instance, say you're at the grocery store, and Max asks you for a candy bar. You tell him no, and he throws himself down on the floor and starts screaming. If he did this at home, you would put him in timeout. But here, people are staring at you, and you're tempted to either yell at him to prove to them that you are handling your child or give in to his begging and attempt at manipulation in order to make him stop screaming and embarrassing you.

With the rise of the self-esteem movement, there are many parents who have become afraid to discipline their kids in public lest they suffer judgment from their peers. Kids are smart. They sense this. That's why they throw tantrums in public—because it works. Mom and Dad cave almost every time, and when Mom and Dad cave after having said no, the child sees that no doesn't really mean no, it means "scream about it, and we'll probably give in." Parents who buckle under the social pressure combined with the desire to make the kid stop being irritating are likely to experience recurring testing and manipulation behaviors in their children.

Max might be all happiness and joy when you give in to his wish for the candy bar, but you can bet that the next time he wants something, he'll throw another fit when asking you for it doesn't yield the desired results.

How Children Use Your Fear of Judgment to Manipulate You

There are many different tactics children use when they want something and you're not giving it to them. Have you ever noticed that when you're around other people, it sometimes seems like they up their game? It's like they intuitively know that you have a burning desire not to be mocked or seen as incompetent by other adults and will be more likely to go to drastic measures to keep from looking stupid or incompetent in front of them.

Dr. Thomas Phelan identifies several of these manipulation tactics that kids use and offers ways of dealing with them that nip them in the bud while minimizing repercussions from other adults.

One of the most common manipulation tactics that a child might use is badgering. This is exactly what it sounds like. "Mom. Mom. Mom. Please can have it? Please? Why not? Why not? Please? Why not?" The rationale is that if he keeps being annoying, you will give in to his demands in order to make him be quiet and leave you alone. As you can likely guess, giving in under the pressure of badgering only reinforces its effectiveness and ensures its future use. Once you've calmly and firmly said no, make it clear that a punishment (like a time out or loss of toys or privileges) will take place if they don't stop asking. Be sure to follow through on the punishment if he continues badgering.

Another all-too-common manipulation tactic is intimidation. This is the tantrum.

Norah throws herself down onto the floor and screams and kicks her legs until you give her what she wants. The more you try to reason with and cajole a child throwing a tantrum, the more you reinforce the intimidation behavior. There are several good options for dealing with this. Tamora, mother of an especially combustible four-year-old says that if she's shopping, she'll often just leave him on the ground in the aisle and continue with her shopping. "When he realizes that I'm not going to give in, he stops his fit and comes and finds me." She said she doesn't ever go more than one aisle over, but also remarks, "I doubt anyone would want to kidnap him with a scream like that." Another punishment you can enforce is a time out. Don't start the time until the tantrum has stopped.

Another manipulation tactic is the threat. You tell Max no cookies for breakfast, and little Max says, "Then I'll run away from home. Maybe I'll just kill myself. I'll eat poisonous worms instead." You might be tempted to be startled and concerned about these threats, but rest assured that there are very few children who mean these things when they say them. You feed him, clothe him, comfort him when he's afraid of the dark, play with him, and give him a constant stream of I love yous. He's mad at you, but when he's not trying to manipulate you, he adores you. Don't be afraid to punish him for making threats. Your wish for him to eat something healthy for breakfast is hardly unreasonable. Send him to time out, or take away his morning treat.

The martyrdom tactic is when a child laments that no one loves her, and she never gets what she wants. Giving in to her martyrdom becomes equated with proof that you love her, which plays with your heartstrings. You don't want her to believe that you don't love her, after all. This is right where she wants you. Like the child who threatens, the martyred child is just trying to get her way. Tell her calmly and firmly that no means no. Time outs and loss of privileges can happen if she continues.

A child might use physical tactics if all else fails in order to get her way. These include breaking things and running away. Dr. Phelan advises that you not clean up the mess immediately. Wait until the child has calmed down and have her help you clean up her mess later. This is a good way to enforce natural consequences. You threw your clothes all over your bedroom, now you can help pick them up and put them away. He states that if your child uses this tactic over the age of four or five, it might be a sign that he needs professional help.

Finally, the butter up tactic is used by your children to make you feel good about yourself right before they ask you for something they suspect you won't give them. Unlike the other manipulation tactics, you don't punish this one. As it's a preemptive tactic, they haven't yet done anything wrong. If they were to butter you up, make a request, and then start badgering, then you should punish them.

The important thing to keep in mind with manipulation tactics is that—shock of all shockers!—they are designed to get you to do things or agree to things that you have already said no to. When used in public, they become the lethal weapons of childhood.

Jodi was at lunch with a friend. She'd told her eight-year-old daughter, Jillian, that if she was good, she could have a friend over this afternoon. Jillian, however, was becoming restless, and Jodi knew that she was bored of the conversation and wanted to go home. "Mom. Mom. Can we go?" she said, interrupting the conversation. "When can we go?"

"We'll go when we're all ready to leave," Jodi said. "Be patient."

Jillian waited a few more minutes. Then she switched tactics. The little girl sighed loudly, and she said, "Well, I guess no one loves me."

"That's enough, Jillian," her mother said. "I do love you, but I'm talking to my friend right now. Remember what we talked about."

A few minutes later, Jillian brought out the big guns right in the middle of the restaurant, "Since you don't care about me anyway, maybe I should just kill myself."

Jodi could feel all of the eyes of judgment turn on her. What a horrible mother she must be to cause her eight-year-old daughter to be suicidal. And she was doing nothing but ignore it. How selfish of her. How dare she discipline a child who clearly has such low self-esteem that she would threaten to kill herself?

Were the people around her actually thinking these things? It's hard to say. If any of them were parents, perhaps they would understand that the threat was an attempt to manipulate her. On the other hand, perhaps they didn't have children and didn't understand this. In any case, it didn't matter. What mattered was Jodi's perception of what they thought of her.

At home, Jodi would have said, "That's three, go to your room. And no friends over this afternoon," Jillian would have grumbled and whined that it wasn't fair, and then she would have found some other way to entertain herself.

Here, at the restaurant, she felt trapped. She didn't want the people around them to think that she abused her child. Moreover, the friend she was having lunch with was looking at her like her kid just said that Mommy beat her.

This is a hard situation, because in some cases, as with Georgiana at the beginning of the chapter, people might jump to extreme, false conclusions and take drastic measures. It sounds ridiculous, but it's a real concern with parents today. News stories of domestic abuse get huge media coverage and leave everyone a little bit more cautious (and in some cases more paranoid) than they were before.

So what do you do when your child manipulates you into an awkward situation in public? Do you save face and give in, or do you discipline her as usual, knowing that there's a possibility someone might call you out on it?

The best answer we can think of in Jodi's situation is to apologize to her friend, and leave right away but remain calm. Once she gets angry and yells at her daughter, she's given in twice to her manipulation and given her control over the situation. She's the parent, so she has to stay calm. When they get out to the car, Jodi tells Jillian that since she didn't let Mom visit with her friend, she doesn't get to have her own friend over later. She should keep it short and sweet. The more she talks and explain her reasoning, the less effective she will be. Jillian's eight. She knows what she did wrong. She was told what would happen if she didn't behave. She had multiple warnings, and she chose not to obey. She must deal with the consequences.

Whatever you choose to do in public situations like this, just know that letting that kind of behavior slide or giving in to her demands will only increase the odds of a repeat incident. Kids are smart. And when a certain manipulation tactic is working, they will keep using it on you to get what they want. As a parent, you know better than they do what they need. You are the boss. Letting them take control is only going to screw them up.

Keep in mind that no parents are perfect. The people judging you won't be perfect parents, and neither will you. People will judge you. It's what they do. But giving strangers, acquaintances, or even well meaning friends too much credence when they criticize you can undermine your parenting and cause you to give positive reinforcement for a behavior that is inappropriate and could get her into huge trouble if she behaves that way toward a person who does not love her.

Think of it this way: disciplining your child yourself when she's in your household means that she's receiving discipline from someone who loves her and wants to make her a better person. Letting her bad behavior slide means that there's a greater likelihood she will be disciplined later on in her life by someone who does not love her or have any vested interest in her self-esteem or future success.

Chapter 13: How Pregnancy Sets The Oxytocin Tone

As the fetus grows in the womb, its development is guided not only by its genes but also by the chemistry of the amniotic bath in which it floats. You could say that the mother's body sends messages to the developing baby via the release of chemicals that are circulating in her body. Remember, at this point, mother and fetus share the same blood via the umbilical cord.

Inside the womb

According to Mitch Gaynor, author of The Sounds of Healing, the fetus is already capable of hearing sounds from outside around the fourth week after conception. Attachment psychiatrist Thomas Verny, author of The Secret Life of Your Unborn

Child, says that as early as the second trimester, the fetus is capable of psychological processing. By the time your baby reaches its eighth and ninth month of life in the womb, he has experienced the world through you on many levels. Your nutritional patterns, your thoughts, stressors, relationships, joys, and concerns create the foundation for the lens through which your child will experience and see the world.

Already, the baby is learning about what kind of a world he'll be born into and live in. The baby's HPA axis, or fear system, is being primed, as is his love and connection system, the oxytocin response.

The idea that a pregnant woman's feelings can influence the way her fetus develops is no longer new-age woo-woo. There's strong scientific evidence that when a woman is stressed out during her pregnancy, her child will later be more likely to have emotional or cognitive problems, including an increased risk of ADD and hyper-anxiety. Scientists aren't sure of the exact mechanism, or of what kinds of stress produce negative impacts on the fetus, but problems in the woman's relationship with her partner seem to be a big factor.

Domestic violence, the loss of her relationship with the baby's father or another important relationship, illness, as well as external events such as being in an auto accident all cause trauma not only to the woman but to her developing baby.

As early as the fourth week after conception, the fetal brain responds to sound, and as early as the second trimester, it displays signs of thinking.

Even if a pregnant woman is in a stable household, relationship or life stress can influence the baby's development.

Co-regulation begins in utero

Remember co-regulation, when two people become attuned and help each other chill out? In a two-parent household, both parents begin to co-regulate not only each other but also the developing baby, as they co-create his emotional environment in the womb and outside. The kind of emotional ecosystem they create begins to affect the child probably from the moment of conception, and it continues to affect the developing fetus until the moment of birth.

To truly parent from love, you must commit enormous amounts of time, energy, focus, and mindfulness until you have reconditioned yourself to dwell in the state more continuously. When you can shift your emotional state from fear to love, your parenting actions and the manner in which you relate to your child will reduce your own stress and that of your baby's.

That's why it's crucial for a couple to work hard to resolve conflicts in their own relationship during this time, as well as to try to come to terms with their own fear. This doesn't mean that every time they fight or get stressed out, they're damaging the unborn baby.

There's Good Stress, Too

In fact, some exposure to stress seems to be beneficial. The cycle of stress/relaxation/stress/relaxation helps build a flexible, adaptable nervous system in the baby.

The key is simply to have an emotional atmosphere that's predominantly positive. Psychologist John Gottman of The Gottman Institute, who studies marriages, found that happy couples say five positive things for every negative thing. This is a good rule of thumb for your oxytocin parenting recipe: Make sure that there's approximately five times as much good stuff in your home life than there is negative stuff.

What If I Adopted My Child?

You may or may not know some details about your child's biological mother and her situation before and during the pregnancy. It's natural for you to worry about how it might have affected the earliest development of your child. Your child's brain is continually changing and making connections for the first three years of life, so this is your opportunity to provide plenty of positive physical and emotional experiences. Skip ahead in this book to the stage at which you brought your child home.

Remember:

☐ Gestation was only the first stage in the development of your child's brain and nervous system.

☐ Much more growth takes place after a baby leaves the womb and enters the world.

☐ There are no "perfect" pregnancies, anyway.

If you do your best to give your child what he needs to thrive — from whenever he enters your family — he has the capacity to develop into a loving, trusting, fulfilled human being. In fact, a 2010 study at the University of British Columbia found that, while highly sensitive children had a harder time handling stress, they also responded more strongly to the support and nurturing of their families than more laid-back kids did.

Action Steps for Pregnancy

1. Visualize: It's natural to wonder what the baby will be like and imagine taking care of her after she's born. Indulge in this behavior as often as you can. Imagine holding, feeding and cuddling her, how happy you'll be and how much you'll enjoy her. Researcher in Israel found that simply thinking about the baby to come can increase oxytocin levels — and pregnant women with higher oxytocin levels felt more bonded to their babies after they were born.

2. Repair Relationships: While you ready your home for the new baby, clean up your emotional household, too. Try to make up with friends right away if you fight; make amends with anyone you've hurt or let down. If you have a spouse or partner, consider some couples counseling or taking a workshop that brings you closer together. Repairing all your relationships has double benefits: It reduces stress — and the stress chemicals circulating in your bloodstream — while increasing your opportunities for enjoying the oxytocin response as you increase your positive social interactions.

3. Add Music: Listening to happy music is one of the easiest ways to elevate your mood. Your positive feelings as you dance, sing along or simply let yourself follow the rhythms transfers to the baby in your womb. The music may have a more direct influence, as well. Because babies are born being able to recognize their mother's voice, it makes sense that your developing baby may be able to respond directly to music.

Chapter 14: How To Build A Connection With Your Child☐

Applying the tips in chapter 3 is much easier to do when you already have a good connection with your child. Positive parenting promotes mutual respect and loving relationships, so building a connection with your child is important. However, it's not always easy to maintain!

For many, modern life is filled with distractions, competing priorities, and too little time. All of these things can get in the way of building and maintaining a strong connection with our family members, including our children. Once they hit kindergarten, they may spend the better part of their days at school and afterschool activities, or friends' houses, while we may be working long hours or fighting to make enough time for all of the important people in our lives, including our children. Without conscientious effort, connections can suffer and family relationships become harder.

A positive connection with your child can help foster their sense of security, independence, and love. It's also satisfying. The parent-child connection can and should be pleasurable to both sides of the relationship, even though both will inevitably experience frustration as well.

In terms of positive parenting, your connection with your little one will help you to be more sensitive to their needs so that you can make better decisions about positive discipline. It will also help you to cultivate a sense of trust with your child, encouraging growth as they feel free to ask for help and experiment in safe spaces.

How you connect with your child – and what that connection looks like – will vary based on their age and developmental progress. Let's take a look at some helpful tips and suggestions for building connection with your little one depending on their age and developmental level. Keep in mind that not everything listed here will work for every child, and some strategies can be applied at more than one stage of development. If you find that a particular suggestion doesn't make sense for your family right now, simply set it aside. It may be useful down the road when your child is older or in a different phase of life.

AGE	Social/Emotional Development	Tips for Connecting
1-2	Increased independence Begins to show interest in new people Begins to show defiant behavior Imitates the	Play simple games together Read to your toddler Talk to her, including asking her to find things or name body

	behavior of others, especially adults and older children Begins to form simple phrases and sentences Follows simple instructions and directions	parts and objects Respond to wanted behaviors more often than you punish unwanted behaviors Encourage him to explore and try new things Take field trips together, such as going to the park Sing to her Give lots of hugs and cuddle time
2-3	Imitates the	Play pretend

actions of others	with your child
Express a wide range of emotions	Go exploring together with a walk or wagon ride
Engages in imaginative play	Encourage your child to tell you his name and age
Shows affection for others	
Begins to engage in turn-taking behaviors	Learn simple songs and rhymes together
Shows concern for others in distress	Play parade or follow the leader
Understands possession, such as 'mine' vs 'his'	Give praise for following instructions, positive behavior, and

	Displays a wide range of emotions Increased independence and willingness to explore without a parent's presence	good choices Make story reading interactive by asking questions about what she sees in the pictures
3-5	Becomes increasingly creative with imaginative play Engages imaginative play with other children Enjoys playing	Do simple chores together Ask your child to recount what they did during the day and what they liked or didn't like about particular

	with other children more than playing alone	activities
		Give your child choices
	Can tell the difference between what's real and what's make-believe more often, but not always	Build simple puzzles together
		Make things together: color pictures or do age-appropriate crafts
	Is able to cooperate sometimes	Sing songs with gestures
	Talks about likes and interests	play more complex games together
	Increased interest in people outside	Be engaged with preschool and kindergarten

	the family Wants to please others Increased independence Increased requests for information as they explore Becomes aware of gender Remembers short stories and songs	activities and homework Have 'date nights,' special outings for one-on-one time with mom or dad Praise her for good behavior, focusing on things she can control (such as choosing to help a sibling) over things that she can't control (such as being smart)
6-8	Increasing independence	Recognize accomplishments

	and confidence when away from parents and family	in school and activities by praising work well done and displaying it in the home
	Thinks about the future.	
	Understands the concept of roles	Talk with her about things she looks forward to
	Friendships become more important	Talk with her about her friends and school
	Can engage in more teamwork	Do kind things together, such as baking cookies and taking them to a neighbour
	Wants to be liked by friends	
	Uses increasingly	Attend fun events together such as movies,

	complex language to talk about their own thoughts and feelings Shows empathy and concern for others	community events, and festivals Take turns reading to each other; when your child reads, ask questions about the story and help him make connections to his life Continue to praise good behavior and choices
9-11	Attention span increases Begins to	Learn something new together Ask your child to

	engage in more complex relationships with friendss and	teach you something they learned at school
	Relationships with friends becomes more emotionally important to have friends	Spend time together
		Ask about her friends
		Ask about her accomplishments challenges
	Starts to experience greater peer pressure	Involve him in helping to make plans for the family, such as planning meals together or setting family goals
	Greater independence from parents and family	
	Can more	Acknowledge

	clearly see the point of view of others	and appreciate accomplishments Continue to make room for one-on-one time and 'date nights,' even though he is becoming increasingly interested in spending time with friends

*Adapted from information found at www.cdc.gov.

In addition to the above age-specific tips, let's take a look at some general suggestions for building connections with your children. Some of these suggestions will help you to create a family environment in which connection can occur, while others are concrete, practical activities you can do with your child to build your connection together.

1. Make family relationships important. Teach your children that family relationships are important and valuable. Verbalize this importance often and reinforce their awareness of themselves as valued members of a family by creating meaningful family traditions, structures, and routines. Make sure to let them know how important they are to the family and how happy you are to have them there.

2. Interact on their level. Make eye contact, get down on the floor with your child, play games that he enjoys, have conversations about things he's interested in. Children can experience a more meaningful connection with you when they feel that you are interested in what they are and when the interaction occurs in ways that they can understand and relate to.

3. Show affection. Don't be shy with smiles, hugs, and positive words. Let your child know that you enjoy being around them, that you take pleasure from their presence in your family, and that you value them. Focus on things that you genuinely like about them, so that they know you love them not just because you're their mother, but also because you enjoy them as people.

4. Apologize. If you make a mistake, model the behavior you would like your children to learn. Don't be afraid to acknowledge the mistake or apologize for it. Doing so can help build a sense of mutual respect between you and your child.

5. Pay attention. It's all too easy get focused on our smartphones, what we're planning for dinner, or the meeting we have at work tomorrow. Sometimes this can't be avoided, but try to put such distractions aside during conversations with your child and give them your full attention. Use active listening to engage with them and show that you value what they have to say.

6. Play together. Children love to play, and playing with them can be a great opportunity to build connection and add to the emotional bank account. Engaging in games like chase, hide and seek, or even getting on the floor to play with toys together will build up positive experiences between you and your child and can be full of opportunities for positive teaching if you look for them.

7. Read stories together. Many children find it calming to sit next to mom or dad and read stories together. Story time can build connection by giving you and your child a chance to share an imaginative experience together. Enhance the experience by asking questions about pictures and ideas from the story, making predictions together, and extending story evens and concepts to your child's real life.

Chapter 15: Positive Parenting With Toddlers

If you are the parent of a toddler, the good Lord knows that some days can be quite a nightmare. Your baby has grown into a toddling, talking miniature version of you, and more often than not, they are driving your bonkers with their mule-headedness. Toddlers can be quite the handful, to say the least. Being a parent of a toddler is all about taking the time to look at the world in their shoes. As a parent, you are responsible for supporting them as they begin to take their very first steps into the world. This chapter is full of discussion on how you can actually enjoy the years of toddlerhood instead of dreading them.

It's time to face the fact that your baby is no longer a baby, but a growing human being. Each day parenting a toddler becomes a little more complex as they absorb more and more of the vast world around them. They are also developing a mind of their own. The contents of this chapter will help parents to encourage good qualities in their toddler(s) that will allow them to flourish as they continue to grow like weeds!

Laying a Healthy Foundation of Emotional Intelligence

Emotional intelligence is critical while raising a kid. It is the umbrella that allows them to properly manage their anxiety, their emotions, fears, etc. In providing them with proper emotional intelligence tools, you are assisting your child in being able to determine their own quality of life. And I am sure you can guess who the person is that emotional intelligence boils down to right? That's right, you! Here are a few tips in laying a good foundation for your child to grow upon:

Hold your child as an infant when they want you. Respond to their cries. High levels of emotional intelligence begin with early interactions. This is when your child develops feelings of trust and security.

Calm your anxiety. Infants, like animals, can detect when you're anxious or worried. The way you move, the way you speak, and the way in which you touch your infant can soothe them or create anxious feelings.

Teach them to self-soothe. Babies, toddlers, and younger children alike are swamped with a variety of emotions. The entire world of all new information comes at them all at once. Imagine your first day at a big job, but with 100 times more sensory information. That is what the world is like for a toddler. This is why as an infant, it's vital for a baby's brain to have parents that meet their needs, for the nerves in the brain that help them self-soothe later on will not develop properly if you don't meet their needs. This will lead to children that act out more later down the line. Do your best to provide calming relief to your child.

Acknowledge their emotions. As a parent, you have every right to set limits to your toddler's actions. You must teach them that they do not have the power to choose how they feel, but they do have the choice to decide what they can do with those feelings when they arise.

Empathize when in doubt. Your child can accept their emotions through your acceptance and empathy. This helps them to resolve and move on from how they feel. Empathy teaches them that the emotional part of life is inevitable but not dangerous. This is vital in letting your kids know they are by no means alone, that emotions are only human and can easily be managed.

Don't distract them from their feelings. Refrain from saying "Big boys don't cry" or "A little scratch cannot hurt." Empathize with them and allow them time to process what occurred. This will help them to move on.

Don't use repression. When you disapprove of your child's feelings, this can give them a reason to bottle them up inside. Repressed feelings do not simply go away, but are trapped and always looking for a way out. This may be the reason why your child is acting out.

Actively listen. Accept, listen, and allow your child to reflect on their feelings. You are then showing them how important it is to truly understand why they feel the way they do.

Help with problem solving. Negative feelings tend to dissipate much faster in all ages of human beings when we feel accepted and understood. Children need the help of parents to help them brainstorm ideas to resolve issues. Do not simply dictate how to handle the issue, but be sure to be there if they ask for your help.

Handle anger constructively. When a toddler is angry, look past the surface. What is this emotion really defending? Toddlers especially learn from what you model. Breathe, become calm and listen.

Model emotional intelligence. Monkey see, monkey do! Do you snap at people randomly often when stressed? Do you have minor fits when things do not go your way? Your child will see this behavior and mirror it.

Don't undermine self-knowledge. Respect your child's feelings in regard to other people. If they are not a fan of Uncle Mikey hugging them, teach them that it's okay to shake their hand. Let them have the freedom to trust their own gut feelings, even if they are merely discomforts that they can not yet identify with. Children need to have room to make their own decisions about relationships, the earlier, the better.

Model discussions about hard topics. Each child has their own set of issues that they may be hesitant to talk about. These are the topics that you should be focused on really discussing, for they often need more guidance in these areas. Overcome any personal discomfort you have about that issue. If you feel guilty, then it will shine through, even to a child. Encourage regular and frequent times that you allow your child to open up to you about whatever topic(s) are on their mind. I recommend bedtime. There is something about the concoction of a dark room, all snuggled up in the covers that allows children to feel comfortable enough to reveal what they are thinking.

Dealing with Tantrums

Tantrums are a legendary norm for toddlers. They can easily get upset since they do not have the capacity in their frontal cortex to control their emotions just yet. Here a few things any parent can do in order to tame the tantrums:

Think ahead. As a parent, you need to firmly instill regular napping, snack, and quiet times. Do yourself a favor and do not drag a hungry or tired kid to the store. Put that errand on a future to-do list.

Reconnect each and everyday. Tantrums happen more often than not simply because your child feels needy.

Acknowledge their anger and what they want/need.

At this age, your child is asserting the fact that they are indeed a person of their own. You don't need to prove you're right to them. Allow them to say no as long as it doesn't compromise their safety.

Remember that:

Toddlers are just beginning the process of experimenting with all of their senses and finding their sense of self. They see themselves as powerful, which can also lead to defiant feelings. This is natural, no matter how frustrating.

Toddlers are determined little boogers, so expect them to be obstinate.

Toddlers are also naturally impulsive, so parents need to keep a close eye so that they don't put themselves in danger.

Toddlers are excited little explorers. The world is a vast place for them, and somehow, they always are getting themselves into situations.

Toddlers, sadly, do not have an off/on switch. This means when they begin to tire, they still keep going until they literally just crash.

Chapter 16: How To Bring Out The Best In Your Child

We have been successful teachers for 30 years and we know that praise and rewards can bring about miracles!

Some people argue against using praise and rewards as they believe that children should be self-motivated and not influenced by external motivation. This can happen if rewards and praise are used in the wrong way, used too often or as a form of bribery.

First of all, let us suggest to you, what not to do.

Be careful never to make the mistake of rewarding every successful experience or achievement. If you do this you'll be causing a huge problem for yourself.

We've all seen this happen. Some children will not do a job around the house unless they are rewarded with money, food, etc. You don't want to raise an ungrateful and unmotivated child.

Poor use of rewarding happens all the time during my son's soccer games. Well-meaning Dads offer their child $5 if they score a goal. Scoring a goal is a team effort and a number of players make it happen. As soon as money is offered as a reward for that particular child scoring, they will not pass the ball and the team performance is diminished. A much better way is when the child comes off the field and they had played a good game, Dad should have told his son, "Wow, you played so well, your kicking is really coming along and I could see that you never gave up when the other team got the ball. I'm so proud of you." He could then further reward his child by either giving him some more of his time or a physical reward, e.g. go the park and kick a ball or buy an ice-cream.

It is important not to always buy rewards for your child every time they do something well, otherwise they will expect this as a type of "payment" for doing well.

We find that praise and rewards are a huge motivator for children. However, they must be earned. Children know if praise is undeserved and if you do this then your child will dismiss all the praise you give, whether it is deserved or not.

Use praise to encourage your child. If you see them doing the right thing, e.g. picking up their mess, trying hard, sharing, being kind or generous, concentrating on a task, using manners etc, then make sure you praise them. As well as kind words, tell them why you like what they are doing, e.g. "You are such a kind girl Sarah, I loved the way you shared your toys with Emma today." "I'm so proud of you James, reading the comments on your report card tells me that you are trying your best at school."

Give praise and rewards for trying their best. Whatever they have done doesn't have to be perfect! If you only praise when something is perfect this may cause the child to become anxious and feel that they aren't good enough resulting in a lowering of self-esteem. We all know adults who felt that they were never good enough for their parents. These kids tend to grow-up and leave home as early as possible and they rarely have a loving and confident relationship with their parents. So don't pressure your children to try to achieve beyond their ability.

Offering rewards for good results on report cards is another potential hazard. Some parents offer financial incentives for grades on their child's report card. We are all different, some children will score an A with little effort and others will give 100% effort and score a C or D.

Be especially careful if you have more than one child in your family. If one is smarter than the other, this can lead to the less intelligent child feeling that the other child is the favorite and they are a failure. We don't recommend giving financial incentives for marks on reports. If your child has done their best and you will be able to judge this by reading the teacher's comments and marks for effort and behavior and their effort during homework time, then by all means give them a reward, but not just simply for how many A's they received.

When we communicate, 93% of the message is in our tone, body language and facial expression. Only 7% of communication is in the words. So when you praise your child, look them in the eye, smile and use your tone to show that you are happy. Then give them a hug, pat on the back, handshake or rub their hair. If your method of giving praise is genuine and loving then it will be much more effective and meaningful to the child.

Give appropriate rewards or praise your child as soon as possible. Make sure the rewards are things that your child will really want and value.

As teachers and parents, we have found it much easier to change negative behaviors when we incorporate praise as one of our strategies. Often naughty or negative kids only hear nagging and negative comments. Of course these poor behaviors can't be ignored, but if you catch your child doing the "right" thing, make sure you praise them and in a way that tells them why you are happy.

We have turned around many children who were considered to be totally anti-social and very poorly behaved. With some children this praise needs to be given in a quiet and private way. A quick pat on the shoulder and a quiet word in their ear is acceptable, as they are not used to being the focus of positive attention in a classroom or a family situation.

Every child is different and you know your child the best, so do what works best for them. By using rewards and praise well...you can really bolster your child's self-confidence and encourage positive behaviors.

Chapter 17: How To Raise A Teenager Right

Teenagers are the most difficult people to handle. It is quite difficult to understand teenagers and even know what they want in life. As a parent, you may do something thinking that it will make your teenage daughter or son happy only to make them unhappy. Parents should be very careful on how they handle their teenage kids.

In order to raise your teen right, as a parent you should

Monitor their company

Most teenagers' behavior is influenced by their peers. If your teenage child is walking with the right group of people, then those people are most likely to impact positively on the life of your teenage child. In the pursuit of getting to know who your teenage child spends time with, you can ask your child to invite their friend over for dinner or even invite the whole family over for dinner. During dinner, you can get to know your child's best friend better. If they are nice people, you will surely discover that during the time you spend together.

If you do not like your child's best friend, you can discuss that when they are gone. You should not bring about the topic when the visitors are around as this will only make your child feel embarrassed and even become mad at you for attacking their best friend. In everything you say or do, be sure to handle your teenage child with great care so as not to trigger their bad side.

Monitor your teenager's performance at school

A child's performance can depict how a child's life is going on as a whole. If your child is not performing well academically (after they have been doing all well in the past), it can indicate that something is bothering them. You should strive to find out what is going on in their lives and deal with it. Maybe your teenage child is a victim of bullying or even is under the influence of drugs. You can try to speak to your teenage child to find out what is bothering him or her.

Sensitize your teenage child on the effects of using drugs

Most parents never speak to their kids about the effects of doing drugs and most teenagers who find themselves in difficult situations try to resolve them by using drugs. If you have not yet talked to your daughter or son about the dangers of doing drugs, then this is the high time you did so.

Tips on how to talk about drug abuse with your teenage child

Discuss with them the dangers of using drugs and the effects of such drugs

If your teenage daughter or son knows the effects of doing them, he or she will never attempt to use them. This is the best way to fight drug abuse among young people.

Teach your child the best ways of dealing with stress

When there is a better way of dealing with stress, they will not resolve to do drugs when they are stressed.

Inquire from your child how he or she feels about people who do drugs

If he or she simply replies that he or she does not see anything wrong with such people, be sure that it will not be that difficult for him or her to join the company of drug abusers. If he or she seems really offended by drug abusers, then he or she will surely not end up using drugs.

How to tell whether your child is doing drugs

As a parent, sometimes your busy schedule may not allow you to spend quality time with your teenage child. You only meet during dinner or on weekends. The following are signs that may indicate your child is doing drugs.

Mood swings: The child becomes irritable and grumpy and then suddenly happy and bright.

Withdrawal from family members: The child who has always been close to his siblings and relatives suddenly becomes distant and withdrawn. Although this may be a sign of other things like stress, you should definitely watch out for it.

The child becomes careless at personal grooming. May be he does not comb his hair or brush his teeth anymore. He evens leaves his room in a mess.

Less interest in hobbies or other favorite activities: He is not interested in the normal things that normal people do.

Red eyes and change in sleeping habits.

Poor academic grades and even misses school or fakes sickness in order to evade school.

Although the signs above are common behaviours among teenagers and may not necessarily mean that your teenage kid is doing drugs, they are a great kick start to help you understand better what your child is up to and by so doing, you will be able to know whether your child is doing drugs.

Things you should not do when you notice that your child is doing drugs

Most parents forget that kids do not do drugs on their own will. Some are too stressed and just do not have someone to talk to. Others just found themselves in the wrong peer groups and ended up doing drugs to fit in their peer groups. If you discover that your child is doing drugs, you should not:

Ignore and decide that the child will find his way out of the drugs just as he found his way into drugs.

Exchange tantrums with him. Remember this child is experiencing a difficult time in life and he does not want to feel like he is the worst. Talk to your child with love and they will surely listen.

Get mad and call him names or tell him that he has destroyed his life. Remember there is nothing that cannot be undone. Handle your teenage child carefully and with love. Most of them do drugs because they feel that no one cares about them. If you show your child how much you care, then he will have something to hold on when all does not go well.

Do not seek relatives help immediately. No one wants to be seen as a failure in his family. Involving relatives will only make him feel embarrassed and may even go back to doing drugs after rehabilitation to psychologically get rid of his embarrassed state. Instead, you should handle his problem by talking to him and seeking to understand why he is doing the drugs. You could even talk to a psychiatrists but ensure to keep the matter a private affair within your nuclear family.

Encourage your teenager

In order to raise your teenager in the right way, you should make sure that you get involved in the activities of their daily lives. Always be there when your child needs you. If you discover that your child has a special talent, maybe he is good at playing a certain instrument like the piano or he is good at singing, do not let his talent fade away. Always encourage him to continue practicing. You never know, he might be the Jay-z or Rihanna of tomorrow. Always help nurture your child's talent.

Talk About Sex With Your Teen

Some parents never talk about sex with their teenagers and this might result to undesirable consequences like early pregnancies and school dropouts. Parents are too shy to talk about sex or just assume that their kids know everything about sex. As a parent, you should teach your child the right time to be intimate. If your beliefs do not permit sex before marriage, then you should teach your daughter or son the importance of abstinence. Most of the teenagers are not aware of their rights and some may even hide about things that happen to them.

The following tips can help you talk to your child about sex

Teach your child to always report to you in case he or she is sexually abused. Being friendly to your child may give him or her courage to confide in you in case of anything.

Be open. Do not hide anything while discussing about sex with your teenage child. Hiding things from your child only worsens the situation and leaves your child with un answered questions

Discuss safe sex with your child. It is definite that your child will be intimate one day. Teach your child on how he or she can have safe sex. You can always buy him condoms whenever you suspect that he or she is intimate with someone. If you are too shy to do this, you can entrust a friend to talk to him or her.

Talk to him or her about sexually transmitted diseases. If he or she is made aware of these diseases, he or she is more likely to have safe sex or remain chaste altogether.

Things not to do if you suspect that your child is intimate with their partner

Quarrel him. Yes! Do not quarrel your teenage child; if he or she did not tell you, then it means that he or she does not trust you. Try to gain his or her trust first.

Demand to meet his girlfriend or her boyfriend. When the right time comes, he or she will surely bring her or him home.

Try to stop them from seeing the partner. If your teenage son or daughter is seeing someone, do not stop them. This will only make things between the two of you hard.

Chapter 18: Difference Between Boys And Girls (Preschooler Level)

Characteristics of boys

·Boys love motion boys and girls were observed over a period of time and it was discovered that boys were very attracted to mechanical motion. They once gave a boy the chance to look at people talking or a fan in motion and the boy chose the fan. Why? Because he was a boy being a boy hehe...

·Boys are more emotional than many people think study shows that boy children get more agitated than girls. If you look at their face you would not notice but when their heartbeat and breathing rate was measured, it showed they were going through more stress than the girls.

·Boys prefer larger groups of people young boys prefer dealing with big groups of people instead of an individual.

·Boys prefer darker colors as compared to girls

·They are more fearless as compared to girls boys fear starts showing at a later age. However, that depends on personality.

Characteristics of girls

·Girls are made to mimic if you have observed young girls, they love playing games that involve role playing

This happens especially in matters revolving around human interactions. Such activities may include taking care of the baby, being mommy and watering the plants.

· Girls are able to utilize their hands girls manipulate their hands faster as compared to boys. They start feeding themselves and using feeding utensils at an earlier age as compared to boys. In class, girls have a good handwriting and learn to write faster.

· Girls are better listeners girls are more attracted to human voices and happen to talk a lot as compared to boys. They get more engaged especially if the stories are interesting.

· Girls enjoy face time Young ladies are more prone to build up and keep up eye contact, and are pulled in to individual countenances—particularly women's.

They also are able to interpret facial expressions without difficulty. For example, if you show them a frightening face, they will be afraid and quickly run to their mommies.

Study shows that boys take longer to recognize facial expressions.

·Girls talk sooner than boys at a very tender age, girls start communicating by use of gestures like waving goodbye, hello, no yes and many others.

When it comes to understanding, girls start understanding what you are saying earlier than boys do. They are also in a better position to start talking at an earlier age as compared to boys.

Chapter 19: Learning Through Play

Toddlers are always at play it seems. While a lot of people feel that play is idle and not very valuable, the truth is, toddlers learn the most when they are playing. The truth is that toddlers are more interested in what they are learning when they are playing, when it is fun. Most parents try to get their toddlers to sit down and learn things and get frustrated when the child gets distracted. This is also when a lot of children get diagnosed with ADHD. Most of the time, it is a misdiagnosis. Toddlers' brains are constantly going, so it is hard for them to focus on one thing for a long time.

If you engage them in mentally stimulating play, you will get them to focus a lot longer than you can get them to focus on worksheets or learning their alphabet from flash cards. Think back to your school days, did you learn better when the exercise was interesting? A lot of times, if you are interested in the information in front of you, you will absorb it a lot better. If you are faced with a boring learning style, your mind will wander.

There are several activities you can do to teach your toddler the alphabet, their numbers, and even basic sight words along with colors and shapes. You can engage your child in play while also teaching them their basics that they need to know before they go into school. You can also teach them their name as well. There is a general list of things that a child is expected to know before they go into Kindergarten. In fact, nowadays, it is expected that these children know how to do these things before they enter preschool, so it is really a pressure on parents to teach their child. The list of things that toddlers should know is as follows.

How to hold and cut with scissors: A lot of preschools do crafts with children, and those crafts require the use of safety scissors. You may be a little wary of a toddler handling scissors, but there are plenty of safe scissors for little hands, and it is better that they know how to handle them before they hurt themselves in school.

How to write their name: Preschools used to have pre-made name tags for their students; however, they now expect children to be able to write their own name. It is to avoid any confusion or mixing up of children in classrooms. Your child also has to be able to write their name semi legibly. It is important that a parent teach their children what their name is and how to write it. This is also great in an emergency if you are not available to answer questions for emergency personnel.

The alphabet: Toddlers are expected to know their alphabet and how to write all their letters. They should be able to recognize both upper and lowercase letters, and they should be able to write both upper and lower case letters. This is a lot different than 10 years ago when children learned that in kindergarten.

Their numbers: Children are now expected to be able to at least count to 10. They are expected to not only be able to say their numbers but also recognize them. They have to know how to point out groups of objects and know how many are in the group. This seems like a lot for a toddler; however, it is what is now expected of them.

Colors: This is a typical thing that preschoolers are expected to know. Colors are fairly easy to teach, as color is everywhere. Children are expected to know both primary and secondary colors. These are the colors Red, Blue, Yellow, Green, Orange, and Purple.

Shapes: Toddlers are expected to know their shapes. Just basic shapes, such as triangle, square, circle, and rectangle. Some schools expect them to know rhombus and trapezoid as well. It all depends on what preschool you will be sending your toddler to.

This may seem like an overwhelming list to teach your toddler because, predominately, the learning will be on you. However, children learn rather easily if you make it fun. This chapter has some activities that you can do with your toddler to get them engaged and help them learn along the way. These also use household objects and fun toys so that you can teach your child without breaking the bank.

Colors

We will start with the easiest thing to teach a toddler. Colors. There are several ways that you can teach your child their colors, and all of them can be fun. Again, all of these are used with typical household items, or cheap craft items. These will not break the bank and can be reusable. Any project that has choking hazards will be noted.

Colored sensory dough

This is a dough that will help your child get some sensory stimulation, along with teaching them their colors. The sensory output will help them focus longer, and they can play with it for a long time. It is also nontoxic, so curious mouths do not have to worry. These are three common ingredients you find in your pantry probably daily.

You need three cups of flour, three tablespoons of oil, and packets of Koolaid in the different colors of red, blue, yellow, green, purple, and orange. If you can't find packets in each color, you may have to mix some primary colors to get the secondary colors, which can also be a good lesson for your toddler. You also need containers to hold the colors in and a big bowl to mix the big batch of dough.

Your toddler can help you make this dough. There is no part of making it that is dangerous. In a big bowl, mix the dough and the oil until it sticks together but feels fluffy. You may need to add a little bit of oil, but the dough should be slightly crumbly, just not dry. It should almost feel like a cloud. Let your child use their hands to mix the dough. Get in there with your hands and mix as well. Laugh and have fun. Then, split the dough into six equal half-cup sections.

Mix the Koolaid into the dough by desired color. Once you have all six colors, take the dough to a play table, and sit down with your toddler. Then ask them to find each color of dough, and identify what color it is. Every time they get the color right, they get to play with the dough for 5 minutes. If they get the color wrong, they have to put it back, and try again with a different color. They will want to be able to play with the dough, so they will be focused. After their time is up, have them put the dough back and try another color.

Lego groups

All you need for this activity are legos. The big ones are best for toddler to use. You want several of each color, including secondary colors if they are available, which they generally are. However, if they are not available, you can teach your toddler how to mix colors to get a secondary color.

Separate the colors into groups of at least five legos. Just like with the dough, if your toddler gets the color right, they get to play with the legos for 5 minutes. If not, they have to try again. If you do not have secondary colors, you can teach your child to point out what two colors you would mix to make that secondary color.

If you can only find small legos, they can be a choking hazard. Likewise, legos can pose a pinching hazard. However, that should not sway you from this activity, as long as you supervise.

Popsicle dip

This is a fun little activity that kids can do. However, it can get messy, but that is just part of the fun for a toddler. Be prepared to give a bath after this activity. This is an activity where you should not be swayed by the mess, but rather, you should embrace it and show your toddler how to have some messy fun. This should only be done in an easy to clean area. Outside is the best.

To do this activity, you need clear disposable cups, Koolaid, water, and popsicle sticks. You may also need a plastic drop cloth or newspaper. A plastic cheap shower curtain would work as well and probably better than the newspaper as this is a wet activity. Find a place in your house or outside to do this activity.

Mix the Koolaid and water in separate containers, and set out the popsicle sticks. Have your child identify colors, and if they identify the color correctly, they get to dip a popsicle stick in that color. This can get messy because they drip, but it's all in fun. If you want to make it more interesting, let them "paint" with the popsicle stick on white paper.

If they do not get the color correct have them try again.

Easter egg extravaganza

This is not only for Easter. You can do it any time of the year, indoors or outdoors. This is a safe activity, and it will help your child not only with their recognition of color but also with their seeking and finding skills. This is also a clean activity, so if you do not have time or the patience to be dirty one day, you can still help them with their colors.

For this activity, you need plastic Easter eggs of each color and snack foods or other treats like small toys to use as a reward for each Easter egg found. You also need some good hiding places as well.

To do this activity, you need to fill each color of egg with a treat or reward, and then hide each color separately. Start with one color, and once they find all those eggs, hide another color, etc. Once they have found all the eggs of each color, let them have their rewards, or if you want to spread it out, let them have a bit of their reward, and then let them have more later.

Shapes

There are not a lot of different ways to teach shapes, but that does not mean that there are no ways to teach shapes. Here are some interesting activities that you can do to teach your child shapes.

Paper jewelry

This is a fun and safe way to teach your child shapes. You can also use this for scissor control if you decide you want to teach your child to use scissors. To do this activity, you need construction paper of various colors (this is also good for a color lesson as well), a hole puncher, some string, and some scissors.

Cut out the shapes, or have your little one do so, and punch holes in the top of each shape. Have your child identify each shape you ask them too, and if they do, they can add it to their string to make a necklace or bracelet. If they don't they have to try again with another color. At the end, they will have a piece of "jewelry" that they made.

Dough shapes

Don't throw away the colored dough just yet! It can be reused for this activity as well. Dough shapes are very fun for the child to play with, and there are many ways that you can do this. The top two are the most fun, so we will stick with those, as the child gets to do the work on the dough without parent interference for the most part.

For this activity, you will need the colored dough and plastic cookie cutters in different shapes. Make sure to at least have triangles, squares, circles, and rectangles. These are the main shapes that toddlers are expected to know.

For the first activity, roll the dough out flat. Ask your child to identify a shape in the cookie cutters. If they correctly identify the shape, allow them to cut out five of those shapes and then play with them for 2 minutes. If they do not get it correct, have them try again with a different shape.

For the second activity, you do not need the cookie cutters. This is for children who have pretty much gotten good at identifying shapes. It also helps develop fine motor skills with their hands. Have your child form the dough into a shape (or close to it). If they get the shape correct, they can play with the dough however for 5 minutes. If they do not, they have to try again.

Alphabet

There are a few fun ways to help your child write their alphabet and identify their letters. Once you teach your child to sing the alphabet, you can teach them to identify and write them with these two activities.

Popsicle stick creations

This is a fun way for kids to learn what their uppercase letters look like, which for most preschools is sufficient. This requires some help from the parents to create them, but it will be fun for the kids as well.

To do this craft, you need construction paper cut into uppercase letters, popsicle sticks, and hot glue. The hot glue is why you will need to help your tot with this project, but only at the very end.

To do this activity, you will show them a construction paper letter and tell them what letter it is. Have them repeat it back to you. Then give them the letter and have them lay out the popsicle sticks on it to make the letter. Once they have laid out the popsicle sticks in the shape of the letter, hot glue them together. From then on, have them use those letters to identify their alphabet. They will be more receptive to learning with something that they created. You can also let them paint the letters if you wish.

Trace paper

This is to help your child write their letters and also identify their letters. It can also help with pencil control. With this activity, it seems like it would be boring, but with bright colors, children seem to be more interested, than with boring tracing worksheets. This requires a little effort from you, but it is worth it to help your child.

For this activity, you will need construction paper cut into letters (several of each letter) and a nontoxic marker for your child. Markers are easier for their little hands to grip, and they are colorful and fun. Have your child trace each letter, and you can even have them find the letter before they trace it.

These are just some of the ways that you can have your child learn through play. There are many other ideas out there, and the important thing is that you engage your child in educational play.

Conclusion

Parenting isn't rocket science. However, parents sometimes make it so hard for each other and the kids such that they end up making life unbearable for everyone. As you have learnt, understanding that each parent has a unique parenting style and a unique place in the upbringing of a child makes a whole lot of difference in finding the right balance that will mold the kids to responsible adults. I hope you have learnt that and are ready to start using whatever you learnt to make your family life worthwhile.

www.ingramcontent.com/pod-product-compliance
Lightning Source LLC
Chambersburg PA
CBHW072008070526
44583CB00015B/1388